THE ESSENTIAL OSBERT LANCASTER

An Anthology in Brush and Pen

THE
ESSENTIAL

BARRIE & JENKINS

LONDON

DAILY EXPRESS

OSBERT LANCASTER

An Anthology in Brush and Pen

Selected and introduced by
EDWARD LUCIE-SMITH

First published in Great Britain in 1988 by
Barrie & Jenkins Ltd
289 Westbourne Grove, London W11 2QA

British Library Cataloguing in Publication Data

Lancaster, Osbert, *1908–1986*
    The essential Osbert Lancaster : an anthology
    in brush and pen.
    I. Title   II. Lucie-Smith, Edward, *1933–*
828′.91209

ISBN 0-7126-2036-2

Design and Art Direction: Ivan Dodd
Layouts: Ian Smith
Phototypeset by Tradespools Ltd, Frome, Somerset
Printed and bound in Portugal by Printer Portuguesa

CONTENTS

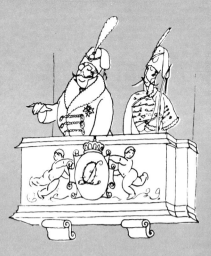

INTRODUCTION

In theory, the British admire all-rounders. In practice, they are suspicious of them, especially if they are good at all the very different things they do. Osbert Lancaster might seem, at first glance, to have been exempted from the consequences of this suspicion. Looking back at his achievement, one sees that this was not, alas, altogether true. I never had the privilege of knowing Osbert personally, though I remember seeing him occasionally in the distance, promenading gently in the company of his wife, Anne Scott-James—she very tall, he rather short. They made a striking couple because of the contrast in stature, and Osbert's memorability was increased by his own carefully cultivated appearance. To describe this, I can't do better than borrow from Robin Young's profile of him in *The Times*, published shortly after he died:

> With his poached-egg eyes, martial moustaches, tweedily dandified clothes and bufferish pose as the last of the great clubmen, he seemed to have stepped out of the magically preposterous world of his own drawings.

But therein, I think, lay the rub. Osbert Lancaster got away with being enormously witty, and also (which is different) enormously perceptive about the wide range of subjects that interested him, while rousing none of the resentment which would have been visited upon a less amiable and—yes—less clubbable man. But the price he paid was that of becoming a character in the seductive fantasy world he invented for the entertainment of the readers of Lord Beaverbrook's *Daily Express*. Looking back on what he did, his cartoons now seem the least important part of his achievement. Even so, they are integral to the rest, connected by many links to his other writings and drawings, and very obviously the product of the same creative personality as the one we discover in his books. The links are both overt and covert. The contemporary representatives of the Littlehampton tribe were Osbert's vehicle for comment on current events. Their ancestors loom large in some of the architectural-cum-historical satires, and also in texts which are pure fantasy, such as the medieval adventure, *The Saracen's Head*. This is so tightly knit that it is impossible to excerpt from it, but it is one of the most perfect *jeux d'esprit* he ever devised.

Osbert's direct ancestor as a caricaturist was Sir Max Beerbohm, who also contributed quite a bit to his style as a writer. Yet there are important differences. Beerbohm tended to concentrate on real personages, for example, the members of the Pre-Raphaelite circle. Osbert made some drawings which are very much in the Beerbohm manner, for example, the scatological but amusing "After Breakfast at Kelmscott", which ventures further into Pre-Raphaelite intimacies than Beerbohm himself would have cared to go. In general, however, Osbert preferred invented personages to real ones—he used to say he drew cartoons, rather than caricatures. The pocket-cartoon format which he used probably derives from the situation-comedies in strip form drawn by Caran d'Ache (Emmanuel Poiré) for the French newspaper *Le Figaro* in the 1880s, but Osbert uses only one frame from the

1

Osbert Lancaster at home.

strip, and leaves the reader to infer the rest. He was able to rely on the reader's response because he carefully built up a cast of characters who could be used to comment on any foible of the day—Maudie, the predatory aristocrat; her baffled husband Willie; their dreadful children; associates such as Canon Fontwater; and assorted gormless or rebellious domestics—cooks, nannies and au pairs. Another technique was to find a number of variations on the same basic theme. Towards the end of the war he rang numerous changes on the flying-bomb or doodlebug. One day it was two angels surveying a third, who consists only of a pair of wings and a halo. The caption is "Look, pilotless!" Another day it was a parrot reproaching a cat: "If you must purr, for Heaven's sake don't cut out suddenly in the middle!"

To readers of the *Daily Express*, his characters took on some of the complexity and solidity of real life. It was possible to imagine Maudie's reactions to many situations which her creator did not choose to illustrate. In this sense Osbert Lancaster was less a traditional caricaturist, in the style of his contemporaries Low and Vicky, and more a kind of novelist manqué. He was sometimes asked to provide jacket designs for certain works of fiction, and it is interesting to note what these were; prominent are the works of Anthony Powell and P. G. Wodehouse. These two names do in fact give a useful indication of his range. Into the pocket cartoons he packed, miraculously, in view of the miniscule scale, many insights: brilliant sparks and flashes which illuminate the evolution of British society as its many layers were torn apart by the strains imposed by the twentieth century. In a more leisurely and detailed way, Powell does the same. But Lancaster also shares P. G. Wodehouse's sense of fantasy, and in particular the latter's keen appreciation of the light that shines, paradoxically, from the reactions and utterances of the ineffably dim.

If there is one writer of fiction to whom one can properly compare him, it is surely Evelyn Waugh. Lancaster lacked Waugh's savagery; and also his misanthropy. But in some respects their stance was similar. Both came from solid upper-middle-class backgrounds. Both were fascinated by aristocratic dottiness, but also by aristocratic powers of survival. Waugh's Agatha Runcible, in *Vile Bodies*, is Maudie's older cousin; Mrs Stitch (whom Waugh modelled on Lady Diana Cooper) is quite likely to have been Maudie's sister or sister-in-law.

It is clear if one looks at Osbert's two autobiographical books, *With an Eye to the Future* and *All Done from Memory*, that his inventions as a cartoonist were in many cases founded on observed reality. One of his most masterly pen-portraits is his likeness of Great-Aunt Martha. What is particularly striking, something which tends to distinguish Osbert from other autobiographers describing characters who made an indelible impression on them in early childhood, is his eye not only for details of appearance but for physical ties:

> The particular gesture of Aunt Martha's which I found so revealing and which, had I not seen her so frequently employ it, I should have come to consider a stereotyped illustrator's convention, no more having an origin in nature than the Fascist salute or the sudden heart-clutching of an Italian tenor, was that with which she invariably registered surprise. This was an emotion constantly evoked in her by the unexpected brilliance (as she thought it) of her great-nephews and nieces or the extraordinary things of which the newspapers were nowadays so full. Maintaining her usual upright but placid attitude when seated, she would suddenly elevate her eyebrows to a remarkable height and in perfect unison raise her hands, which had been lying quietly in her lap,

The Tenor, *Friends of Covent Garden Magazine*, with a costume design for the chorus of *La pietra del paragone*.

MANHATTAN
AFTERNOON

HERE those of us who really understand
Feel that the past is very close at hand.
In that old brownstone mansion 'cross the way,
Copied from one that she had seen by chance
When on her honeymoon in Paris, France,
Mrs. Van Dryssel gave her great soirées;
And in the chic apartment house next door
J. Rittenhaus the Second lived—and jumped,
The morning after General Motors slumped,
Down from a love-nest on the thirtieth floor.
Tread softly then, for on this holy ground
You'd hear the 'twenties cry from every stone
And Bye-Bye Blackbird on the saxophone
If only History were wired for sound.

'Manhattan Afternoon' is the first of a series of
illustrated poems which will be found
throughout the book. They appeared together
as a poem sequence in *Façades and Faces*.

6

One of the characteristics of Osbert Lancaster's work was its immense variety, not so much of style as of mood and subject matter. He evolved a very personal graphic language which could express a wide range of different ideas. Its sources included Baroque art, the topographical drawings of Edward Lear, and Victorian and Edwardian caricaturists—George du Maurier as well as Max Beerbohm.

Osbert was fortunate in being offered book jacket commissions which exactly suited his temperament and interests. On the opposite page is a cover for *The Ambassador* magazine.

smartly at right angles to her wrists with palms outward, at the same time, but more slowly, lifting her forearms till the tips of her outspread fingers were level with her shoulders, in a manner perfectly familiar to me from the illustrations of Cruikshank.

I make no apology for quoting this passage at some length, because it also gives a very good idea of the distinctive quality of Osbert Lancaster's prose style. This is at first acquaintance quite surprising. Though not as elaborate as the manner developed by Sir Osbert Sitwell for use in his own volumes of autobiography, it has a steady, slightly Latinate march which seems at variance with the quickness and accuracy of the perceptions which the soundly carpentered clauses enshrine (the Latinity is more a matter of structure than it is of actual vocabulary). Clearly this style was created as a matter of deliberate and conscious choice, like the persona which Osbert himself presented to the world. If one turns to early writings, such as the pen-portrait of King John which appears in a long-forgotten book called *Our Sovereigns*, one sees that he had originally been attracted to what one might call the Lytton Strachey manner:

> Of all our kings John had probably the least to recommend him. As cruel as Richard III, as lecherous as Henry VIII, as untrustworthy as Charles I, and as ineffectual as Stephen, his sole redeeming feature seems to have been that, like so many celebrated criminals, he was invariably kind to his mother.

His later manner is much more Augustan than this. If one may hazard a guess as to how and why Osbert came to evolve this style, it can perhaps be put down to his complex relationship to the culture of the Victorian age. His prose is a Victorian means of communication, adapted to modern purposes. By the time he came to write his autobiographical volumes, Osbert Lancaster was keenly aware of his good fortune in having experienced at least the lingering afterglow of the Victorian epoch. Born in 1908, he was one of those people who retain detailed recollections of their earliest years, for example of the delights of being wheeled along in an old-fashioned perambulator. He was a London child, and his descriptions of London life just before the First World War are bathed in a golden glow:

> How different it all was in the years before 1914! Then the stucco, creamy and bright, gleamed softly beneath what seems in reminiscence to have been a perpetually cloudless sky. Geraniums in urns flanked each brass-enriched front door, while over the area railings moustachioed policemen made love to buxom cooks. And in every street there hung, all summer long, the heavy scent of limes.

This was the direction in which nostalgia led him. The Victorian-Edwardian age was a lost paradise, which he had been fortunate enough to glimpse. His intellectual attitudes towards the Victorians, and towards their aesthetic achievements in particular, were more ambiguous. During the 1920s, that is during his impressionable adolescence, Victorian buildings, paintings and artifacts were out of favour with "aware" people, intellectuals and anyone who prided themselves on having advanced taste. It was only here and there, especially among a circle of Oxford undergraduates, that one saw signs that the tide was beginning to turn. These took up Victoriana as a joke at the expense of their immediate elders, then discovered that it repaid serious study. Osbert, who arrived in Oxford at the end of the 1920s, seems to have started to analyse the Victorian achievement in architecture

---

Jacket design for the only book on which Osbert Lancaster collaborated with his second wife, Anne Scott-James.

at that time. His enthusiasm for it was reinforced by the poet John Betjeman, who was a fellow undergraduate and who became a lifelong friend. It was strengthened still further by Osbert's association with the *Architectural Review*, from 1934 to 1939.

In a way it is ironic—given the ambiguity of the impulses which drew him to it—that the way in which we now react to Victorian architecture owes so much to the way in which Osbert Lancaster both described and depicted it. His combination of skills, as a writer and as a draughtsman, made him a uniquely vivid and pithy commentator on architecture of all kinds. He was later to demonstrate his expository skills with much more esoteric subject matter: the architecture of Byzantium.

Basically, one can see three rather different attitudes at work in Osbert's most ambitious, and also most influential, architectural compendium, *Here of All Places*. The book uses a very simple format: a full-page drawing of a building or an interior (all, as the author explains, imaginary) facing a page of expository text. In dealing with the "classic", non-controversial architectural styles, Ancient Greek to Regency, the thrust is to explain: simply, lightly, accurately, and if possible with a spice of wit. These pages still provide one of the quickest and least painful ways of gaining some kind of architectural education. The twentieth-century section is largely satirical, and expresses the author's scorn of both modern and revival styles, as used and misused by twentieth-century builders and decorators. The pages given to the nineteenth century are a good deal more complex. Here, too, there is a satirical edge, reinforced by Osbert's gift for coining memorable descriptive phrases; "Le Style Rothschild" and "Pont Street Dutch" have both entered the language, the latter so completely that everyone has forgotten its origin. But the categorisations are much subtler than the twentieth-century ones. Some highly original thought has gone into them and they make it possible to get to grips with certain aesthetic phenomena which were nebulous before Osbert found ways of portraying them.

During the period when Osbert Lancaster was most closely linked to it, the *Architectural Review* was involved in exploring the idea of "vernacular architecture", that is, the kind of building which was not necessarily the work of a major architectural figure, but which nevertheless seemed to sum up the essence of a period. In fact, such buildings might not even be the work of trained architects at all. Osbert himself clearly saw architecture in these terms, as a sociological phenomenon, expressing wishes and fantasies of which its creators might be quite unconscious. The great architectural names appear in his writings rather seldom, and very much in passing. He thus had nothing to do with the scholarship of recent decades, which has made a detailed examination of the careers of Victorian hero-figures such as Pugin, Butterfield and Burges. But the context within which we see their work still owes a great deal to Osbert Lancaster's idiosyncratic reassessment of the Victorian achievement.

His enthusiasm for vernacular building styles (he particularly liked the wall decorations to be found on Irish Victorian pubs) may have been one of the things which led him to the study of Byzantium. The builders of most Byzantine churches are anonymous; the constructions are often small; the plan and arrangement of architectural elements is more often than not irregular. While Byzantine studies are often made to seem impossibly esoteric, the buildings themselves are very direct. Furthermore, the Byzantines are linked to the Victorians, whom Osbert already knew well, by a taste for intricate pattern.

But there was much more to it than this. Osbert first got to know Greece when he was attached to the British embassy in Athens at the end of the Second World War. The country was having its own civil war at the time, and a few scenes from this are described with his customary vividness in *Classical Landscape with Figures*. Typically, it is an outré architectural setting, Skaramangar House, a "perfect example of Hollywood Balkan", which inspired him to one of his best flights, a description of an encounter with Archbishop Damaskinos:

> Without the night was stormy, and the sound of heavy firing was carried on the wind from the direction of Pankrati, muffling from time to time the cries of the sentries challenging the occasional passer-by; within, all the electricity in the city having long since failed, the only illumination came from a roaring log-fire in the immense, heraldically-canopied open grate and an excessively ecclesiastical candelabra standing on a refectory table. In a throne-like chair by the fire I could discern the robed immensity and noble beard of the Regent-Archbishop; behind him the gold lace and buttons of the Evzone in full uniform shone and twinkled in the firelight. Somewhere in the shadows lurked a liveried footman in white cotton gloves. At any moment, I felt, the Princess Flavia would, with incomparable grace, come down the wide staircase, passing that curtained alcove which, for all I knew, might well conceal the redoubtable Rupert himself.

Though he wrote dutifully about the Athenian Acropolis, Olympia, the temple at Bassae and other classical remains, Osbert's heart lay elsewhere, with the relics of the Byzantine Empire, deserted or half-deserted fortress towns like Mistra and Monemvasia; and most of all, perhaps, with the modern inhabitants of Greece, about whose foibles he writes with such enormous relish, tinged with his customary irony. The shift in taste we find reflected in his books about Greece was not peculiar to himself; it was common to a new generation of intellectual philhellenes, who got to know Greece, not through a standard classical education, but directly, as a result of the travels and adventures of the war.

Greece had a more decisive effect on Osbert's art than it did on his writings. Osbert had a full professional training as an artist, at the Byam Shaw, the Ruskin and the Slade, and he was by no means incapable of working on a large scale, as can be seen from his murals illustrating Max Beerbohm's *Zuleika Dobson* at the Randolph Hotel in Oxford, and also from his fine mural in Shell-Mex house. But, like many other English artists of merit, Thomas Rowlandson and William Blake among them, Osbert was essentially a draughtsman rather than a painter. This is one reason why he seems isolated. Additionally, his celebrity as a caricaturist has tended to cut him off from the milieu in which his art was formed, and it is therefore worth asking oneself what parallels can be drawn with his contemporaries.

He can most easily be placed among a group of English artists whose merits are only now being reassessed. For example, he seems to have been influenced by two men just a little older than himself, Edward Bawden (b. 1903) and Eric Ravilious (1903–42). Both were extremely active in the 1930s, when Osbert was beginning his career. Both had been pupils of Paul Nash at the Royal College of Art. What they did was to regularise Nash's somewhat erratic style, turn it into a visual language with its own reliable grammar and use it for all kinds of practical purposes, in step with the then prevalent conviction that art ought to be the servant of society and make itself quietly useful. Bawden was as active as an illustrator and a graphic designer as he was as an independent painter. He designed advertisements for the Westminster Bank and Shell-Mex, did posters for the London Underground, created borders for the Curwen Press, decorations for earthenware produced by Wedgwood, and produced designs for wallpapers and textiles. Ravilious engaged in a similar range of activities: in addition to making designs for Wedgwood, he did glass for Stuart Crystal and furniture for Dunbar Hay Ltd. Osbert's work at this period was almost as varied, and he too worked for some of the most enlightened patrons of the time, the Curwen Press and the London Underground in particular.

One of the things which distinguishes this group of artists is their somewhat sceptical attitude to Modernism. They knew about it, but they preferred their own techniques. Some very early paintings and murals by Osbert show he dabbled in Cubism, more specifically, the rather loose, late version of it practised by Georges Braque in the inter-war period. But he soon gave it up, retaining only a liking for the floating, overlapping planes of colour which the Cubists had devised as a means of controlling pictorial space. But he used this trick so discreetly that its origin is difficult to spot in his fully mature drawings.

Osbert was influenced more directly and visibly by his close connection with the magazine *Architectural Review*. In a general sense this kept him informed of everything new in the field of interior design and the visual arts, and he became adept at taking what he needed from any new trend, always putting his borrowings into the visual quotation marks supplied by his vivid sense of the ridiculous. This habit linked through to what he took from Bawden and Ravilious, a visual language of signs, which they had originally elaborated on the basis of hints taken from Paul Nash. Yet Osbert could not use even this without transforming it to suit his own purposes. The Augustanism of his prose-style also found its way into his draughtsmanship. His linear structures are consistently more closed and regular than those of his exemplars.

The final decisive influence of his art was his experience of Greece, Greek buildings and the Greek landscape. These had the effect of making him more adventurous, and far more conscious of the importance of the contrast between concentrated pattern and blank space. The impact of Hellenic light becomes everywhere apparent, perhaps most of all in the coloured drawings, which tend to contrast absolutely plain surfaces, scrubbed clean by the light itself, with areas of intricate texture. One artist from whom he may have borrowed some hints as to how to deal with Greek subject matter was his friend Nico Ghika (b. 1906). Ghika, trying to make painting which would appear both acceptably modern, and at the same time truly Greek, made an intelligent exploration of folk sources, such as the intricate embroideries worked by Greek women in the nineteenth century and later.

Osbert's talent was from the start theatrical. His cartoons show miniature dramas, caught at some moment of resolution or crisis. One of the collections of pocket cartoons which he brought out is actually called *Theatre in the Flat*. Similarly, the architectural drawings always have something rather stage-like or stagey about them. This comes from two things. One is the way in which characteristic features are cunningly heightened and dramatised. The other is more specific: his rooms, and indeed his exteriors, often look as if they were built up from stage flats (these flats are, in fact, also the residual planes which Osbert took over from Cubism). It is not surprising that he received many invitations, from the 1950s onward, to design for the stage.

His first stage success was John Cranko's ballet *Pineapple Poll* in 1951, and thereafter his designs were mostly for opera and ballet. Some of the best-remembered productions are Stravinsky's *Rake's Progress* (1953), Verdi's *Falstaff* (1954), Rossini's *L'italiana in Algeri* (1957), and Ashton's ballet *La Fille mal gardée* (1960). It can be seen from this that he was almost invariably confined to the lighter side of the repertoire, perhaps because producers felt that a professional cartoonist could not cope with anything more serious.

David Hockney, who is (surprisingly) Osbert's most obvious successor in the theatre, may initially have struggled under disadvantages of much the same kind, but has recently made his escape and has been entrusted with Wagner's *Tristan und Isolde*. One wonders what Osbert would have made of such a project; he did *Peter Grimes*, in its own way a serious enough piece, for the Bulgarian National Opera in Sofia in 1964. It is in any case fascinating to note that Osbert and Hockney were asked to tackle some of the same works—Stravinsky's *Rake* and Poulenc's *Les Mamelles de Tiresias*. In the Stravinsky piece, their approach was very similar, partly because both kept Hogarth very firmly in mind.

Osbert, in his lecture on stage-design, printed in this book, I believe for the first time, stresses the common-sense aspect of stage-design, and also its collaborative nature. There is another aspect he might have mentioned, the fact that good stage-design is essentially didactic: it helps to explain the nature of the piece to the audience. This, as much as the fact that it is a sociable, communal kind of activity, is probably why it appealed to Osbert. Of all his gifts, his gift for exposition and explanation has been the most neglected.

Many people love Osbert's work for its elegance, its wit, its good humour, its lack of pretension, its "bubbling sense of fun". I have no wish to deprive them of the Osbert they know, he is represented in full measure in this book. It is only just to point out, however, that he possessed a didactic talent of the first order, which was the mainspring of many of his activities. *Sailing to Byzantium*, for example, contains what is perhaps the clearest exposition of Byzantine architectural style and its special properties ever devised; I say "devised" because it depends in equal measure on words and drawings in order to make its points. One also finds this side of him at work, perhaps more openly than usual, in the essay on conservation (or, as he dubs it, "preservation") which began life as an address to a seminar held at Williamsburg, Virginia, in 1963. One of the things that particularly appeals to me about this piece is its logical defence of sentiment, what Osbert preferred to call "piety" (the choice of word betrays his classical bias):

> By piety I mean, in its application to architecture, an emotion widely diffused, unaesthetic and comprehensible only in the light of a people's proper consciousness of their past. In many cases, perhaps, the buildings which evoke it will justify their continuing existence also on aesthetic grounds, but not always. Take, for instance, the Tower of London or Paul Revere's house in Boston. To a detached view the former is simply an injudiciously restored, rather provincial example of twelfth-century functionalism, less offensive than the powerstation across the way because smaller and unselfconscious; the latter an easily matched example of colonial domestic dwelling. But nevertheless, any threat to either would arouse a nationwide storm of righteous indignation. Such a reaction is in my view right and proper; and, responding to some of the deepest feelings of the human race, is not to be dismissed as pure sentimentality. How moving, still, are the few monolithic pillars of the Temple of Hera which the Greeks, the least sentimental of peoples, piously left untouched in the very centre of Olympia where every generation did its best to outstrip its predecessors in the scale and sumptuousness of its rebuilding!

This, with its combination of moderation, good sense, logic and feeling, does honour to the man who wrote it. To me it is just as representative of the Osbert Lancaster I know through his writing, and through his work as a visual artist, as are the many delicious jokes with which the pages of this anthology are strewn.

16

No one ever rivalled Osbert Lancaster in his nostalgic evocation of the Edwardian epoch. The mounted knight on the facing page comes from the card on which he responded to congratulations on his knighthood. One of the minor satisfactions of this honour must have been that it gave his already striking combination of names a rolling period ring.

AUTOBIOGRAPHY

Osbert Lancaster's autobiographical books, *All Done from Memory* and *With an Eye to the Future*, contain his finest prose. The Overture in *All Done from Memory* has particular resonance. There are longer books of memoirs, often by more widely celebrated contemporaries such as Sir Osbert Sitwell, which cover much the same territory, but few are more perfect works of literary art, and it seems likely that Osbert Lancaster's contributions to the genre will survive as classics. They are important to the student of the whole body of his work because they record the deep impact made on him of direct childhood experience of the world before the First World War. The sights and sounds of this lost realm are recreated with tremendous clarity. I have also made a point of including Osbert's character study of his mother, which deals chiefly with a later epoch, because this so well illustrates the affectionate detachment of his lifelong study of human character.

JUST A SONG AT TWILIGHT

Overture from *All Done from Memory*, 1953

I CANNOT honestly say that my attitude to flying bombs was ever one of gay insouciance. Nevertheless as they grew more frequent I developed a paper-thin tolerance which I had never achieved during the earlier, more orthodox, bombardment. For one thing there was not, after the first few days, any anti-aircraft fire, which brought two advantages: first an unaccustomed quiet, and second, and more important, a welcome freedom of movement. During the "blitz" so long as I remained indoors I was ceaselessly assailed by what psychiatrists so unfeelingly describe as "irrational fears", but on escape into the wide open spaces these were promptly transformed by the patter of shrapnel into anxieties to which my reason accorded every justification. But during the short summer nights of 1944 it was possible to cut short the long hours of bedroom terrors by escaping into streets unmenaced by our own defences. And so it came about that on such evenings as I was not on duty I developed the habit of taking long walks through the misty Kensington evening and exploring districts which had for so long aroused my curiosity as to have acquired an almost fabulous quality but which in ordinary times I had never had the opportunity, or had lacked the energy, to penetrate.

The Holland Road which leads northward from my house is not in itself a romantic thoroughfare but the backdrop framed by the wings of its long stucco perspectives had always had for me a certain sinister fascination. A circular building in the style that the Mid-Victorians were pleased to call Palladian marks the entrance to a narrow street of cheap shops running into the main road at an acute angle, crowded in peacetime with stalls and costers' barrows, which had always from earliest childhood strangely affected my imagination. In part this was due to an occasion when my father had, as a great treat, taken me to the White City Exhibition and we had halted here on our return to enjoy the spectacle of the seething Saturday night crowds, the women all in tight sealskin jackets and vast plumed hats, the men in pearl-buttoned waistcoats and flared trousers, jostling round the street market in the theatrical light of the gas jets; in part to the mystery and surprise which always colours any sudden revelation of a crowded slum life existing behind a pompous and familiar façade and which is as powerfully induced by suddenly coming on one of the tenement streets which emerge between the neo-Renaissance palazzi of Fifth Avenue as by the half-glimpse of the Venetian ghetto seen beneath the arch of the Merceria. Here, moreover, the romance had been much heightened by the fear and distaste for the neighbourhood beyond, to which the more nervous of my elders were accustomed from time to time to give whispered expression. For in my youth Notting Dale was held, not, I fancy, altogether unreasonably, as one of the most dangerous districts of London and it was confidently stated that it was impossible for a well-dressed man to walk the length of the Portobello Road and emerge intact.

So powerfully had the prevailing attitude reacted on my subconscious that, although I had never in fact had occasion to do so, I had never gone out of my way to investigate this Alsatia of North Kensington. Now, when it seemed probable that the more enterprising thugs would be exercising their calling, thanks to the favourable conditions provided by the blackout in the profitable districts of W. 1., and the more nervous would be deep in the Tube shelters, was surely the ideal time for this long-postponed exploration.

The deeper I penetrated into this stucco wilderness, deserted save for an occasional pathetic figure weighed down by bedding hurrying through the drizzle to the Shepherd's Bush Tube Station, the more insistent did the past become. A certain plenitude of frosted glass and bold Victorian display types, still characteristic of Dublin and the lower East Side of New York, but elsewhere in London long since submerged beneath a flood of chromium plate and modernistic sans-serif, was doubtless chiefly responsible, but in addition long-buried memories of streets half seen in the distance from my pram, as Nurse cautiously skirted the fringe of this City of the Plain on our way to Wormwood Scrubs in the hope of seeing Mr. Grahame-White go up in his new flying machine, played their part. As I drifted on in a vaguely north-eastern direction, ears cocked for overhead chugging, the sense of familiarity deepened and finally achieved its maximum intensity at the end of a curving street of dilapidated semi-detacheds, all peeling paint and crumbling volutes.

As I paused to take in this panorama of decay my attention was irresistibly, but apparently illogically, drawn to a house immediately opposite across the street. Separated from the pavement by a few square feet of trampled grass and sooty laurels, the brickwork of the low wall still bearing scars that marked the recent outwrenching of railings for the armaments drive, it in no way differed from any of its neighbours; the pillared portico and debased but still classical mouldings marked it as having been originally intended for some solid family of the Victorian *bourgeoisie*; the marked disparity of the window curtains on the various floors, all subtly different in their general cheapness and vulgarity, indicated that it now sheltered three or perhaps four separate establishments. My glance travelling disdainfully across this depressing façade, marking the broken balustrade above the cornice, the hacked and blackened lime trees, the half-erased 79 on the dirty number of the door pillars that had once been cream, came finally and shockingly to rest on the street name attached to the garden wall—Elgin Crescent. This, I suddenly realised, was my birthplace.

In my subconscious eagerness to prolong my evening stroll, I must have walked right through the haunted district I had set out to explore and emerged into the once familiar playground of my childhood on the slopes of Notting Hill. The fact that I had done so all unawares, that I had passed the formerly so firmly established boundary line without for a moment realising it, spoke far more clearly of what had happened here in the last thirty years than could many volumes of social history. As I walked on up the hill, regardless for once of a flying bomb now following the course of Ladbroke Grove seemingly only just above the chimney pots, I noticed with a certain proprietary satisfaction that the progress of decay had not been halted at Elgin Crescent; that the squares and terraces that had once formed the very Acropolis of Edwardian propriety grouped round the church had suffered a hardly less severe decline. Some of the most obvious signs of degradation were certainly the result of five years of war and common to all parts of London, but here this enforced neglect was clearly but a temporary acceleration of a continuous process. The vast stucco palaces of Kensington Park Road and the adjoining streets had long ago been converted into self-contained flats where an ever-increasing stream of refugees from every part of the once civilised world had found improvised homes, like the dark-age troglodytes who sheltered in the galleries and boxes of the Colosseum. Long, long before the outbreak of war these classical façades had already ceased to bear any relevance to the life that was lived behind them; the eminent K.C.s and the Masters of City Companies had already given place to Viennese professors and Indian students and bed-sitter business girls years before the first siren sounded. And yet I who was only on the threshold of middle age could clearly remember the days when they flourished in all their intended glory. At that house on the corner I used to go to dancing classes; outside that imposing front door I had watched the carriages setting down for a reception; and in that now denuded garden I had once played hide and seek.

Many times since that wet wartime evening I have pondered on the implications of the dismal transformation then so suddenly brought home to me. This was not, it seemed to me, just a case of a once fashionable district declining slowly into slumdom but rather the outward and visible sign of the disappearance of a whole culture; a disappearance, moreover, which no one seems to have noticed and for which no tears have been shed. For it is a curious fact the term "upper middle class" used as a social classification should only have achieved its maximum currency at a time when the class, or rather the cultural pattern which it established, had completely vanished; that while all the other labels which attached to the social stratifications of late Victorian life retain in varying degrees a certain relevance, this which is shiny from overuse by leader writers and social analysts marks a completely empty drawer. The aristocracy and landed gentry, although Nationally Entrusted and sadly Thirkellised, are still, thank goodness, for all their constant complainings of extinction, visibly and abundantly there; the lower middle class is not only still with us but so enormously increased in numbers and influence as to impose its own colour and standards on our whole civilisation; the working class, although, anyhow in London, being rapidly reduced by the ever-increasing rate of its absorption into the lower middle class and steadily losing much of its peculiar character remains numerous and powerful. But the old upper-middles, insofar as they possessed a definite culture and set of values of their own, are as extinct as the speakers of Cornish.

It is customary to explain this disappearance either in terms of the Marxian dialectic or by reference to the immense burden of taxation which weighed on them more heavily than on any other section of the community. It can also be correctly maintained that the continuous process of social assimilation, based on a deep-rooted national instinct that bids us reject on the one hand the transatlantic vision of the equality of man and on the other all the continental foolishness of *Ebenbürtigkeit* and sixty-four quarterings, has been immeasurably accelerated in the last fifty years. Whereas a couple of generations separated the medieval burgher from the Tudor squire and another couple intervened between the Tudor squire and the Stuart nobleman, in recent years the social barriers between class and class, which though always clearly marked were never happily insuperable, have often all been leapt in a single lifetime. But although there has always been a two-way traffic, of the probability that only a very small proportion of the two and a half million direct descendants of John of Gaunt would not now be black-balled for a suburban tennis club, economic arguments remain as partial an explanation as dialectical materialism.

Far and away the most important single factor leading to the complete collapse of the upper-middle-class way of life was the invention of the internal combustion engine; for the coming of the motorcar made possible the "week-end", and the week-end spelt doom. However formal may have been the religion of this section of the community, the whole pattern of their life, anyhow in London, yet centred round the church, and once the cohesive force exercised by "Morning Prayer" became weakened by the disruptive influence of the golf links and the week-end cottage the whole social organism collapsed into its individual units. Curiously enough one of the few who seems at the time to have been aware, doubtless purely intuitively, of what was afoot was His late Majesty King George V (always temperamentally far closer to the upper middle class than the aristocracy), for if we are to believe the memoirs of his eldest son, one of the chief of his many objections to the younger generation was based on their fondness for leaving London at week-ends.

The vacuum involuntarily created by Lord Nuffield and his peers was filled in two ways, of which only one was connected with the process of dissolution. The lure of the country, besides ruining the home counties, created a new class whose way of life, although originally based in intent on the emulation of that of the landed gentry, was in fact far closer to that of the middle class immediately below them. By the thirties the differences dividing the £10,000 a year stockbroker from his £800 a year clerk were all quantitative not qualitative. One lived in a gabled mansion standing in its own grounds at Sunningdale, the other in a semi-detached villa at Mitcham, but both residences were bogus Elizabethan and both householders caught the 8.28 every morning. The stockbroker had a six-cylindered Rolls and a Lagonda, the clerk a second-hand Morris, but both were as likely as not to spend Sunday on the golf links. They saw the same films, listened to the same radio programmes, read the same newspapers, and neither of them went near a church except to get married. The way of life of both was equally far removed from that of the stockbroker's father living in Egerton Gardens or Orme Square.

The second, and perhaps more extraordinary, of the twentieth-century inventions which remoulded English social life was that of the intelligentsia. Hitherto, this amenity so long established on the Continent had here been lacking. In Victorian times writers and artists, save for one or two of the most exalted, living remote and inaccessible on private Sinais in the Isle of Wight or Cheyne Row, had conformed to the pattern of the upper middle class to which most of them belonged. Matthew Arnold, Browning, Millais, were all indistinguishable in appearance and behaviour from the great army of Victorian clubmen, and took very good care that this should be so. The *haute Bohème* did not exist and the Athenaeum rather than the Closerie des Lilas shaped the social life of the literary world. Only at the very end of the century amidst the gilded mirrors of the Café Royal did there emerge a society which bore some faint resemblance to those which had long been flourishing in the life of Paris, Vienna and Berlin; and even this, by the equal importance that sporting peers and racing journalists—the "Pink 'un" world in fact—enjoyed along with the artists and writers to whom they were linked by such liaison figures as Phil May and a common devotion to the music hall, bore a peculiar British stamp.

By the time the twenties were halfway through the whole picture had completely changed. The immense increase in size and circulation of newspapers and magazines, the rapid development of the cinema industry, the coming of the B.B.C., the colossal expansion of advertising, and later, the establishment of such organisations as the British Council, had transformed the pocket *Vie de Bohème*, which flourished in the late nineties into a vast army of salaried culture-hounds, an army which recruited its main strength from the younger generation of the upper middle class.

Unlike all the earlier class divisions the intelligentsia forms a vertical rather than a horizontal section of the community. Connecting at the top with the world of artistic dukes and musical minor royalty it trails away at the bottom into the lower depths of communist advertising men and *avant-garde* film directors. But however different the social and financial standing of the various grades within the group may be, the pattern of their existence remains strangely consistent and utterly at variance with that of the old middle class from which so many of the members sprang. Where the parents, even those in some way connected with the arts, lived in substantial houses in which they ate regular meals, the children live in flats and eat at snack bars and restaurants; while the fathers not infrequently tended to look rather overdressed in the country the sons invariably appear underdressed in the town. A society which was predominantly Anglican with a handful of high-minded agnostics has been transformed into one which is predominantly agnostic with a handful of not so high-minded Roman Catholics. For the transformation is widespread and complete. So successfully was the New Bohemia glamourised by female novelists during the twenties and thirties that its way of life has gladly been adopted by thousands of the old upper-middles whose connection with the arts is non-existent. Thus even so late as twenty years ago one was fairly safe in assuming that any bearded figure in corduroys reading the *New Statesman* was at very least a photographer or a museum official, whereas now he is just as likely to be a chartered accountant or a dry-salter. In a world where only Guards officers and bookmakers still maintain a sartorial standard, the social ideals of Murger are everywhere triumphant and even ordained ministers of the Established Church do not hesitate to advertise their broadmindedness with soft collars and grey flannel "bags".

Although the effects of the change did not become generally apparent until after the first German War it was, in fact, well under way by 1914; but due largely to the patriarchal organisation of my family I was the fortunate victim of a time lag and in the halls of my youth there still flourished a way of life which in more sophisticated circles was already in visible dissolution. From the death of the old Queen until the outbreak of war this small society upheld the standards of Victorianism with the same unruffled tenacity with which the Sephardic community at Salonika persisted in speaking fifteenth-century Spanish; fully aware of Bernard Shaw, Diaghilev and Alexander's Ragtime Band their outlook remained as resolutely unmodified by these phenomena as that of the Adobe Indians by the airplane and the radio.

The present volume is not, therefore, primarily autobiographical in intent but rather, by using thematic material drawn from a few commonplace incidents of childhood, an attempt to raise not a monument but a small memorial plaque to a vanished world. Many of the principal characters may well appear to readers below the age of forty ridiculous, maladjusted and anachronistic, wilfully blind to the great changes going on about them and rashly presumptuous in their firm convictions. Such a view is easily justifiable and, indeed, is one which I myself frequently expressed in my heedless youth. But, sheltering from the chugging menace overhead in the shabby ruins of their citadel scrawled with slogans demanding a Second Front and scarred by blast yet still retaining in the evening light an almost Venetian grandeur of decay, self-confidence waned. Whether their disappearance is an irreparable loss or a welcome deliverance I am too close to them to say: I can only record that I have become increasingly conscious of the debt, which, for good or ill, I owe them.

TAKE ME BACK TO DEAR OLD SHEPHERD'S BUSH

Taken from *All Done from Memory*, 1953

I WAS BORN in the eighth year of the reign of King Edward the Seventh in the parish of St. John's, Notting Hill. At that time Elgin Crescent, the actual scene of this event, was situated on the Marches of respectability. Up the hill to the south, tree-shaded and freshly stuccoed, stretched the squares and terraces of the last great stronghold of Victorian propriety: below to the north lay the courts and alleys of Notting Dale, through which, so my nurse terrifyingly assured me, policemen could only proceed in pairs.

The Crescent, like all border districts, was distinguished by a certain colourful mixture in its inhabitants, lacking in the more securely sheltered central area, grouped in this case round the church. While residence there was socially approved and no traces of "slumminess" were as yet apparent, there did cling to it a slight whiff of Bohemianism from which Kensington Park Road, for instance, was quite free. Of the residents several were connected with the Stage, and some were foreign, but neither group carried these eccentricities to excessive lengths. Among the former were numbered a Mr. Maskelyne (or was it a Mr. Devant?) who lived on the corner, and, right next door to us, the talented authoress of *Where the Rainbow Ends*, whose daughter, a dashing hobble-skirted croquet player, remains a vivid memory. The foreigners included some Japanese diplomats and a German family connected with the Embassy, whose son, a fair, chinless youth, was always at great pains to model his appearance on that of the Crown Prince Wilhelm, much to the delight of my father whom a long residence in Berlin had rendered expert in detecting the subtlest nuances of this elaborate masquerade. Fortunately my parents' arrival at Number 79 had done much to erase the principal blot on the fair name of the street, as our house had previously been the home of no less equivocal a figure than Madame Blavatsky.

Number 79 was a semi-detached stucco residence on three floors and a basement with a pillared porch, not differing stylistically in any way from the prevailing classicism of the neighbourhood. At the back was a small private garden opening into the large garden common to all the occupants of the south side of Elgin Crescent and the north side of Lansdowne Road. Such communal gardens, which are among the most attractive features of Victorian town-planning, are not uncommon in the residential districts of West London, but are carried to the highest point of their development in the Ladbroke estate. This area, which was laid out after the closure of the race course that for a brief period encircled the summit of the hill, represents the last rational, unselfconscious piece of urban development in London. It was unfortunately dogged by misfortune, and the socially ambitious intention of Allom, the architect, and the promoters' was largely defeated by the proximity of an existing pottery slum in Notting Dale, which received, just at the time the scheme was being launched, an enormous and deplorable influx of Irish labourers working on the Great Western Railway.

How different it all was in the years before 1914! Then the stucco, creamy and bright, gleamed softly beneath what seems in reminiscence to have been a perpetually cloudless sky. Geraniums in urns flanked each brass-enriched front door, while over the area railings moustachioed policemen made love to buxom cooks. And in every street there hung, all summer long, the heavy scent of limes. The angel who drove the original inhabitants out of this gilt-edged Eden, not with a flaming sword but by a simple vanishing trick, was the domestic servant. The houses, even the small ones like ours, were planned on generous lines and labour-saving was still not only an unrealised but unthought-of ideal. Fortunately my parents whose joint income at the time of my birth amounted to all of £600 a year were able to maintain a cook, a housemaid, a nurse and a boot boy; my mother, moreover, had been through the hard school of a Victorian grandmother's household, and herself undertook such specialised, and now obsolete, labours as cleaning the chandeliers, washing the rubber plant and superintending the linen.

The ideal of the servantless civilisation, already fully realised in the United States, is doubtless a noble one, and those who so bravely, and possibly sincerely, maintain that they feel degraded by being waited on by their fellow human beings compel our admiration, although personally they invariably provoke me to confess that I can tolerate without discomfort being waited on hand and foot. But it is an ideal attended by one grave disadvantage—whom is there left for the children to talk to? A mother's love is all very well, but it is only a poor substitute for good relations with the cook.

In my own case, the centre of the below-stairs world was Kate the housemaid. This remarkable woman, gaunt, near-sighted and invariably prepared for the worst, not only endeared herself to me by acts of kindness to which I could always be certain no strings were attached, but also provided my only contact with the real world which lay beyond the confines of my isolated nursery. Quick-witted and an omnivorous reader of the popular press, it was her habit to converse largely in political slogans and popular catch-phrases. Thus when I was detected sliding unobtrusively into the larder she would call out "Hands off the people's food," and if when driven out she suspected that I still retained some loot she would advance with simulated menace, jabbing the upturned palm of her left hand with the index finger of her right, in a gesture which a dozen cartoons of the then Chancellor of the Exchequer, Mr. Lloyd George, had rendered universally familiar, exclaiming "Put it there!" And always when I asked what was for dinner she would remind me of Mr. Asquith and bid me "Wait and see." But by no means all of her sources of verbal inspiration were political; better even than the Harmsworth Press she loved the music hall, and her evenings off were regularly spent at one or other of the many suburban houses then still happily flourishing on the sites of future Odeons. Her favourite performers were Wilkie Bard, George Mozart and Alfred Lester, and while engaged on her endless scrubbing and dusting she could usually be heard informing the household that she had got a motto, or wanted to sing in opera, or desired to be taken back to dear old Shepherd's Bush.

The popular music of the Edwardian era played an important role in the national life: these music-hall songs and ballads have today been so weakened and degraded by intensive plugging and self-conscious revival over the air that they are now as far removed from their former spontaneous popularity as are the careful prancings of latter-day Morris dancers from the village revels of the Elizabethans. In the strictly stratified social world of my childhood they seemed to me in my bourgeois pram to be the one thing enjoyed in common by the world represented by the whistling errand-boy and the ladies I occasionally observed,

humming gaily, if a little off key, as they emerged from the glittering paradise of *The Devonshire Arms* (in passing which my nurse always developed an additional turn of speed and on which she would never comment), and the world of which the pillars were Kate and my father. I specify my father rather than my parents as his taste was almost identical with Kate's (he perhaps rated Harry Lauder a little higher than she did), whereas my mother's was more accurately represented by "Traümeri" and "Songe d'automne", beautiful works, doubtless, but hardly with so universal an appeal.

A few additional figures there were who stood in a rather closer relation to the small world of Number 79 than the anonymous ranks of passers-by I observed from my pram: they, while obviously debarred from the full club privileges of Kate, the cook, my parents and the boot boy, yet enjoyed, as it were, the facilities of country membership. The Italian organ grinder, a martyr to gastric troubles, who regularly appeared every Thursday afternoon; the crossing sweeper in Ladbroke Grove whose function the internal combustion engine was even then rapidly rendering as decorative as that of the King's Champion; the muffin man, the lamplighter and the old gentleman, who came out on winter evenings to play the harp by the foggy radiance of the street lamp—Dickensian figures who have obviously no role to play in the Welfare State and have left no successors. Doubtless their disappearance should be welcomed, and yet they did not appear to be either downtrodden or exploited: indeed, the impression they gave was chiefly of a proper consciousness of the important role in the social fabric played by muffin men, lamplighters and organ grinders. Certainly their spirits seemed higher and their manners were undoubtedly better than those of the majority of the present-day beneficiaries of enlightened social legislation. Even the crossing sweeper, despite his ostentatious rags and traditional whine, displayed a certain individuality and professional pride which one seldom observes in the hygienically uniformed Municipal Refuse Disposal Officer.

Apart from such figures, my relations and, later, fellow-pupils at my kindergarten, the most vivid and indirectly influential personality of my early childhood was our next-door neighbour to the west, old Mrs. Ullathorne. This imposing and always slightly mysterious *grande dame*, with whom I was bidden to tea at regular intervals, represented an era which, even at that date, seemed almost incredibly remote. She had enjoyed, so it was said, a considerable success at the court of Napoleon the Third, and there were prominently displayed amongst the palms and bibelots of her crowded drawing room innumerable *carte de visite* size photographs of dashing cuirassiers in peg-top trousers sporting waxed moustaches and elegant lip beards, and of crinolined beauties who had somewhat surprisingly elected to put on full ball dress and all their diamonds for a good long read, of what appeared from the binding to be books of devotion, seated on rustic benches in a vaguely Alpine landscape. Certainly Mrs. Ullathorne herself gave a very definite impression of belonging to another, and far more sophisticated, world than that of Edwardian Notting Hill. Alone among all our female acquaintances she was heavily and unashamedly made-up (even the dashing daughter of our playwright neighbour, who was thought to be a Suffragette and known to smoke, never, I fancy, went further than a discreet use of *papiers poudrés*). But the style in which her maquillage was conceived proclaimed her way behind, rather than daringly ahead, of the times. The whole surface of her face was delicately pale and matt, and only by imperceptible degrees did the pearly white take on a faint rosy flush above the cheekbones; the eyebrows, which although carefully shaped were not plucked thin, were a deep uncompromising auburn, contrasting very strikingly with the faded parma violet of the lids. Her toupet, a rich mahogany in colour, was dressed in tight curls and fringes in the manner of the reigning queen. The whole effect was one of extreme fragility which, one felt, the slightest contact or even a sneeze would irretrievably wreck, and was as far removed from that achieved by modern methods as is a Nattier from a Modigliani.

Whether due to Mrs. Ullathorne's long residence in foreign parts or to her extreme age, she displayed another peculiarity which set her still further apart from the rest of my world—she invariably insisted that in place of the customary handshake I should bow smartly from the waist and kiss her hand. This was for me always rather an alarming ordeal, and I can still see that long white hand delicately extended, crisscrossed with the purple hawsers of her veins standing out in as high relief as the yellowish diamonds in her many rings, and experience once more the ghastly apprehension that one day, overcome by unbearable curiosity, I should take a sharp nip at the most prominent of those vital pipelines.

The influence which the old lady exercised on my early development was not, however, direct, but the result of a gift. One day she presented me with a large quarto volume bound in dark green leather into which, with incredible neatness, she had in childhood pasted scraps.

Although I can still vividly remember the enchantment which was renewed every time I opened that magic volume, it is only quite fortuitously that its peculiar flavour, recognisable if faint, now and then returns to me. No effort of conscious memory will work the miracle, but just occasionally the sight of swans upon a castle lake, or some peculiar combination of Prussian blue and carmine, or the feel beneath the fingers of the embossed paper lace on an old-fashioned Christmas card, will play the part of Proust's Madeleine and fire the train. Many must have received such volumes in childhood, but not many I fancy so perfect an example of the genre as this; for the artists of no age have ever surpassed those of the romantic period in the production of keepsakes and *culs de lampes*, and this volume had been compiled at exactly the right moment. The shakoed, hand-coloured infantrymen, who so gallantly assaulted that vaguely oriental stronghold, were the soldiers of Louis Philippe subduing the fierce Goums of Abd-el-Kader; this mysterious steel-engraved lake shadowed by twilit mountains was Lamartine; and the rather overplumed knights, their armour gleaming with applied tinsel, were undoubtedly setting out for the Eglinton Tournament.

The charm and excitement of those vividly coloured vignettes must have made a powerful appeal to the imagination of any child but in my case it was reinforced by the contrast they provided to the illustrations in my other books. My mother suffered from that perpetual illusion common to all parents that the books which had meant the most to her in her own childhood (or possibly those which, later in life, she had persuaded herself had then been her favourites) would awaken a similar delighted response in her offspring. My nursery library was therefore well stocked with the illustrated fairytales of the late seventies and early eighties. It cannot be denied that the skill of the great nineteenth-century school of English wood engraving was then at its height and that many of these volumes were, in their way, masterpieces. Nevertheless, not only did I dislike them all with the solitary exception of Tenniel's *Alice*, but certain of them awoke in me feelings of fear and revulsion.

I do not think, looking back, that my reaction was purely personal nor wholly abnormal. Children are all firmly in favour of representational art up to a certain point (my lack of enthusiasm for Walter Crane, for instance, was caused by his tendency to subordinate accurate representation to decorative embroidery and was of a wholly different kind to my dislike of Linley Sambourne), but that point is reached when realism is carried over into the third dimension. They will welcome, and indeed demand, the maximum amount of realistic detail provided it is flat, but once an artist starts to give his illustrations depth and to visualise his figures in the round, his preadolescent public will begin to lose interest. Thanks to the incredibly responsive instrument which such figures as the Dalziels had made of the wood engraver, the book illustrators of the eighties were able to exploit the third dimension, which still possessed in this medium the charm of comparative novelty, to their hearts' content, and they certainly made the most of the opportunity. The buxom flanks of the Water Babies sprang from the flat page with a startling illusion of rotundity; the more unpleasant creations of Hans Andersen's imagination displayed a devastating solidity; indeed, certain artists went rather too far in their three-dimensional enthusiasm and overstepping the bounds of realism achieved an effect which can only be described, in the strictest sense of the word, as surrealist. In our own day this irrational element in the wood-engraved illustrations of the late nineteenth century, against which I as a child had unconsciously reacted (in exactly the same way, incidentally, as did my own children some twenty-five years later), has been recognised and skilfully utilised for his own terrifying purposes by Max Ernst in such works as "Le Lion de Belfort" and "La Femme à Cent Têtes".

Thus the world of Mrs. Ullathorne's scrapbook, with its brilliant green lawns and flat improbable trees peopled by kindly gendarmes in enormous tricornes and little girls in pork-pie hats and striped stockings practising archery in château parks, took on in addition to its own proper attraction the welcome character of a safe retreat from that other, boring yet terrifying, world of all too completely realised fantasy.

The work from which, next to the scrapbook, I derived the greatest enjoyment was

also uncontemporary, being two bound volumes of the *Picture Magazine*, to which my father had regularly subscribed during his school days at the very end of the Victorian age. This admirable periodical nicely combined instruction with amusement, and among the regular features were a series of simple pseudo-scientific experiments (a cock mesmerised into following a chalked line with its beak and a daring criminal escaping from Vincennes by means of a home-made parachute), accounts of travel and exploration (whiskered tourists being hauled up to the monasteries of the Meteora in nets), and, best of all, strip cartoons by Caran d'Ache. In addition were included from time to time four-page supplements of photographs of the most distinguished figures in one particular walk of contemporary life—soldiers, scientists, painters. . . . Of these my favourite was that devoted to the rulers of sovereign states who, thank Heaven, were at that date far more numerous than they are today.

Those long rows of royal torsos adorned with every variety of epaulette, plastron, and aiguillette, the necks compressed into collars of unbelievable height and tightness, the manly, if padded chests hung with row upon row of improbable crosses and stars and crisscrossed by watered silk ribbons and tangles of gold cords, surmounted by so many extraordinary countenances adorned with immense moustaches, upstanding in the style of Potsdam or down-sweeping in the style of Vienna, some fish-eyed, some monocled, some vacant, some indignant but all self-conscious, had for me a fascination which never failed. And nor, when I had learnt to read, did the captions prove a disappointment; such names as Mecklenburg-Schwerin, Bourbon-Parme, Saxe-Coburg-Gotha held for me a flavour of high romance to which the very difficulty of pronouncing added rather than detracted. How drab by contrast did the still small handful of republican presidents appear, and how deep was my contempt for those pince-nezed, bourgeois figures to whom a gaudy silken diagonal across their stiff-shirted bosoms could not lend an air of even spurious distinction!

Incredible as it may seem, many of these paladins who now appear far more remote from our modern experience than Attila or Ivan the Terrible were actually still more or less firmly on their thrones at the time when I first grew familiar with their appearance. The whiskered porcine features of Franz Josef were still regularly revealed to his loyal Viennese as he drove every morning through the Hofburg; hardly a day passed without his German colleague, dressed as an Admiral, a Hussar, a Uhlan, a Cuirassier, or a Highland sportsman, making an appearance in the illustrated papers; and somewhere hidden away in the heart of the plaster mazes of Dolmabaghchesh, that last bastard offspring of a frenzied rococo which had reared itself so surprisingly on the shores of the Bosphorus, apprehensive, invisible but undoubtedly there, was Abdul the Damned.

Of all this I was at that time naturally unaware. All these characters were no more and no less real to me than Jack the Giant Killer and the Infant Samuel of whom my mother was accustomed to read aloud, or Hackenschmidt and the Terrible Turk, in whose exploits the boot-boy took so keen an interest. Only Kaiser Wilhelm was for me in any way, and that very remotely, connected with real life; for I had once been sent a box of toy soldiers by an old friend of my mother, who was one of that monarch's A.D.C.s, and whose photograph in the full-dress uniform of the Prussian Guard stood on the piano.

Less colourful but more familiar were the pages devoted to the more prominent contemporary divines. No flourishing moustachios nor jewelled orders here, but every variety of whisker from the restrained mutton-chop to the full Newgate fringe, and billowing acres of episcopal lawn. At the time these portraits were taken the social prestige of the

Establishment, and even, on a different level, of Nonconformity, was at its height, and although it had become a little dimmed in the intervening years it was still comparatively great. How complete has been the subsequent eclipse, a brief study of the representative novels of high life during the last half century will amply demonstrate; although the regiments of handsome curates, worldly Archdeacons and courtly Bishops who thronged the pages of late Victorian fiction thinned out a lot in Edwardian times, a sharp-tongued Mayfair incumbent or two, ex-curates doubtless of Canon Chasuble, still make a regular appearance in the tales of Saki; but in all the works of Michael Arlen I cannot recall a single dog collar and the solitary cleric to appear in the novels of Mr. Waugh is Fr. Rothschild, S.J.

In real life, anyhow in the society in which my parents moved, the clergy still played a prominent and honoured role. Their merits as preachers were eagerly discussed and the exact degree of their "Highness" or "Lowness" keenly debated. Many of the originals of those portraits were, therefore, quite familiar to me by name as being preachers under whom members of my family had at one time or another sat, while on the knees of one of them, Prebendary Webb-Peploe, a celebrated Evangelical preacher from whose well-attended Watch Night sermons the more impressionable members of the congregation were regularly carried out on stretchers, I myself had once had the honour of being perched.

It may seem strange that my infant literature should have been so exclusively out of date, but at that time the modern renaissance of the children's book was in its infancy, and the prevailing standard of contemporary productions was unbelievably low. Exceptions there were, however, and I can vividly remember the pleasure I derived from the *Nursery History of England*, illustrated by that happily still flourishing artist, George Morrow, and, a little later, from the works of Edmund Dulac.

To the enjoyment of the pictures, appreciation of the text was soon added, as thanks to the brilliant educational methods of my mother I learned to read at a very tender age. Her system, simple as it was effective, was based on a chocolate alphabet. This was spread out twice a week on the dining-room table and such letters as I recognised I was allowed to eat; later, when my knowledge of the alphabet was faultless, I was entitled to such letters as I could form into a new word. Although never strong in arithmetic I soon grasped the simple fact that the longer the word the more the chocolate, and by the time I could spell "suffragette" without an error this branch of my education was deemed complete and a tendency to biliousness had become increasingly apparent.

Once my ability was firmly established I read everything on which I could lay my hands, from *The Times* leaders to the preface to the Book of Common Prayer. The impressive zeal was not, I fancy, the result of any exceptional thirst for knowledge, but rather of boredom, and was far commoner among children at that time than it is today. Such cinemas as then existed were regarded by my parents as undesirably sensational and notoriously unhygienic, and there was no compulsion on grown-ups to make any pretence of enjoying the company of the young who were, quite rightly, expected to amuse themselves. The only addition which modern science had made to the sources of infant pleasure available to my parents, or even my grandparents, was the gramophone. On this archaic machine I was permitted, as a great treat, to listen to the exaggeratedly Scots voice of Harry Lauder, just audible through a barrage of scratching and whining, singing "Stop your tickling Jock", or to the waltzes of Archibald Joyce rendered, rather surprisingly, by the Earl of Lonsdale's private band and recorded on discs half an inch thick by Messrs. William Whitely.

My appearances in the drawing room, where the gramophone was kept, were deter-

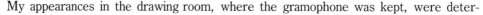

mined in accordance with fixed rules, as indeed were those of almost all the children of my generation—on weekdays half an hour before going to bed and half an hour in the morning to practise my scales, the latter period being prolonged to an hour on Tuesdays when Miss Pearce, poor long-suffering woman, came to wrestle with my highly personal rendering of "The Merry Peasant". Apart from these daily occasions, the only times when the room knew me were when there were visitors.

The pattern of social life in archaic Bayswater, and all points west, differed almost as much from that prevailing today as it did from that of mediaeval times. Fixed rules prevailed governing the exact hours and days on which visits took place, the number and size of the cards left and when and how they should be "cornered", the clothes to be worn, and the length of time which one was expected to stay; even such trivial gestures as those with which the ladies, once perched on the Edwardian Hepplewhite chairs, were accustomed to throw back their veils and roll down their gloves at the wrists, were formal and standardised. There was no casual dropping in for drinks, as drinking between meals was confined exclusively to the restorative masculine whisky and soda (or among the older generation "a little b. and s.")—almost exclusively, for curiously enough I do recollect among certain of my older female relatives the ritual partaking of a glass of port wine and a slice of plum cake at eleven o'clock in the morning, although this was generally regarded as an old-fashioned survival only to be justified on grounds of old age or a delicate constitution. There was no ringing up and asking people round for a little cocktail party as we had no telephone and cocktails were still unknown, save perhaps to certain rather "fast" Americans—the sort of people who patronised those "tango teas" of which the papers spoke.

Where no casual appearance could possibly take place, and all was fixed and preordained, I knew exactly when the summons to present myself below would come. My mother, like all the ladies of her acquaintance, had her Thursdays, when the silver teapot and the best china would be shiningly conspicuous and her friends and relations would dutifully appear to be entertained with cucumber sandwiches, *petit fours*, slices of chocolate cake and, in winter, toasted buns. Those who could not come, either because the number of their friends who had also chosen Thursday as their "At Home" day precluded a personal appearance at each or for some other valid reason, sent round their cards.

My own entry was always carefully timed by Nurse to coincide with the moment when the teacups, with which I was hardly to be trusted, were already distributed and the sandwiches and cakes were waiting to be handed round. My performance on these occasions was invariably masterly. Clad in a *soigné* little blue silk number, with Brussels lace collar and cut steel buckles on my shoes, in which I had recently made my first public appearance as a page at a wedding in All Saints, Margaret Street, I passed round the solids in a manner which combined efficiency with diffidence in exactly the right proportions. Moreover, although conspicuously well behaved, I could always be relied on to go into the *enfant terrible* act at exactly the right moment, and produce embarrassing questions or comments of a laughable kind that yet just stopped short of being offensively personal or too outspokenly apt. The freely expressed admiration which my performance always produced was almost as gratifying to me as it was to my mother, particularly in such cases where I considered it was likely to pay a handsome dividend next Christmas. Only among my Lancaster relations was the rapture apt to be a little modified; my Aunt Hetty, for instance, was more than once heard to remark that if Mamie were not careful dear little Osbert

would soon be developing a deplorable tendency to "play to the gallery".

The only other times (apart from the many-coursed dinner parties of the period, a fixed number of which my parents were accustomed to give during the year, which naturally affected my life not at all) on which visitors appeared was when country relatives were in London and were of sufficient age or importance to be asked to tea or luncheon for themselves alone. The most memorable of these was my Great-Aunt Martha, not only for her own personality and appearance which were remarkable enough, but also for the manner of her arrival. Having been born early in the reign of George IV she was relatively fixed in her ways, and when she came to stay with her younger brother, my grandfather, the victoria and the greys were put at her disposal: their use in London had otherwise come to be increasingly abandoned in favour of the Renault, and they were only still maintained, I fancy, out of respect for Mundy, the elderly coachman, and a deep-rooted enthusiasm for harness horses which was general in my father's family.

I can still recall the stately dignified clop-clop, quite different in rhythm from that of the brisk single-horsed baker's van or the heavy proletarian tattoo of the pantechnicon, which announced that Aunt Martha was rounding the corner, and which I had been eagerly awaiting at the nursery window for half an hour or more. Quickly snatching up some lumps of sugar from Nurse, I was down the stairs and at the horses' heads almost before the footman was off the box. Looking back, I confess myself lost in admiration at my youthful temerity, as nowadays my reluctance to go fumbling round the muzzles of relatively unfamiliar quadrupeds would hardly be so easily overcome.

Great-Aunt Martha, although even older than Mrs. Ullathorne, gave no such impression of fragility; on the contrary she appeared, and indeed she was, exceedingly robust and just about as fragile as well-seasoned teak. Her eyebrows which were thick as doormats were jet-black and her hair, which she wore severely parted in the middle and swept smoothly down over each cheek, was only streaked with grey. She never appeared abroad save in the prescribed Victorian uniform for old ladies—black bonnet enriched with violets, a black jet-trimmed shoulder cape and very tight black kid gloves—which was becoming increasingly rare even at that date and now only survives among pantomime dames. Her features were strong and masculine and bore a close resemblance to those of Sir Robert Walpole as revealed in Van Loos' portrait, and she retained a marked Norfolk accent. Tolerant and composed, she radiated an air of genial and robust common sense, which none of the rest of the family displayed, anyhow in so marked a degree; and alone of all the Lancasters she professed a keen interest in food and was reputed to be the finest hand with a dumpling between King's Lynn and Norwich. In addition she was never at any pains to conceal an earthy relish for scandal which, linked to a prodigious memory, made her a far more entertaining, and quite possibly a more accurate, authority on the genealogies of most Norfolk families than Burke.

Despite her outward Victorianism, Great-Aunt Martha nevertheless always gave a strong but indefinable impression of belonging to a still earlier era. This must, I think, have arisen largely from her gestures, for gestures remain the surest and least easily eradicable of all period hallmarks. Tricks and turns of speech are good guides but are generally indetectable when combined with a strong regional accent; clothes and hair styles may be deliberately and consciously adopted for their period value; but gestures are easy neither unconsciously to lose nor deliberately to acquire. One has only to compare the most accurate reconstruction of a twenties scene in a modern revue with a thirty-year-old film to appreciate this truth; no matter how skilfully the accents and fashions of the epoch may have been recaptured on the stage the film will always reveal a dozen little gestures—a peculiar fluttering of the hand or some trick of standing—which at the time were so natural as to be completely unnoticeable, and of which even the most knowledgeable spectator with an adult memory of the period and the keenest eye for detail will have remained completely unaware and may even, on seeing them again after a lapse of thirty years, fail to realise are the very hallmarks of that genuineness of which he is nevertheless completely convinced.

The particular gesture of Aunt Martha's which I found so revealing and which, had I not seen her so frequently employ it, I should have come to consider a stereotyped illustrator's convention, no more having an origin in nature than the Fascist salute or the sudden heart-clutching of an Italian tenor, was that with which she invariably registered surprise. This was an emotion constantly evoked in her by the unexpected brilliance (as she thought it) of her great-nephews and nieces or the extraordinary things of which the newspapers were nowadays so full. Maintaining her usual upright but placid attitude when seated, she would suddenly elevate her eyebrows to a remarkable height and in perfect unison raise her hands, which had been lying quietly in her lap, smartly at right angles to her wrists with palms outward, at the same time, but more slowly, lifting her forearms until the tips of her outspread fingers were level with her shoulders, in a manner that was perfectly familiar to me from the illustrations of Cruikshank.

Such visits as those of Aunt Martha were, however, few and far between, and the rhythm of our daily life, monotonous as it would seem to a modern child, was but seldom interrupted by these intrusions from the outside world. Thus the drawing room saw me chiefly in its familiar everyday dress, very different from the unnatural spruceness and formality it assumed on social occasions, and so it remains in my memory. Summoned down for my daily visit I would take my accustomed place beside my mother for the evening reading. My enjoyment at this performance depended in a very large measure on the choice of the book, which was governed partly by the day and partly by my mother's mood.

On Sundays and holy days, or on occasions when some recent display of temper or disobedience on my part was thought to have merited implied reproof, the volume chosen was a ghastly selection of fables, illustrated in that wood-engraved style I so much abominated. What particularly infuriated me about the author, and still infuriates me, was not so much his unctuous style, nor even the pious nature of the themes, but his abominable deceit. The hero, some gallant knight, would don his armour, leap on his trusty steed and go galloping off in pursuit of dragons in the most approved style, and then, just as my interest was getting aroused, it was revealed that the armour, on the exact style and manufacture of which I had been excitedly speculating, was the armour of Righteousness, the steed one learnt answered to the name of Perseverance, and the dragons against which the hero was off to do battle were called Self-Love, Indolence and Bad Temper. Thus one cold puff of piety instantly and irrevocably shattered the warm colourful world of romance and fantasy which had been building up in my imagination, and my rage, though concealed, was boundless. But it was years before the sight of that thick little royal blue volume, so guileless and optimistic is the infant mind, warned me to expect the worst.

But in the course of time my so evident lack of response led to the gradual abandonment of this depressing volume, and the occasions on which I was firmly removed from the study of some illustrated volume of my own choice to listen to the far from hair-raising adventures of some smug paladin of evangelical piety became fewer and fewer. And in the picture which I chiefly retain of these early evenings of my childhood it plays no part.

The firelight is gleaming and flashing from the polished brass of the heavily defended hearth; on one side sits my father, freshly returned from the city, reading one of the pastel-coloured evening papers of the time; on the other my mother, studying with well-founded distrust the double-page spread of the interior of the newly launched *Titanic* in the *Illustrated London News*. The pleasantly depressing strains of "The Count of Luxembourg", rendered of course by the Earl of Lonsdale's private band, faintly echo amidst the shiny chintz and gold-mounted watercolours, speaking of a far distant world of dashing Hussars and tight-waisted beauties in long white gloves with aigrettes in their golden hair, forever dancing up and down some baroque staircase of exceptional length. While in the middle, flat on his stomach, lies a small boy of engaging appearance poring over an enormous green volume, the faintly dusty smell of the fur hearthrug heavy in his nostrils, perfectly happy counting the medals stretched across the manly chest of the Hereditary Prince of Hohenzollern Sigmaringen.

THE AUTHOR'S MOTHER
Taken from *All Done from Memory*, 1953

THE first German war was not yet over when my mother decided that that conflict was not, as she had previously supposed, Armageddon but merely a trial run, and that the vials of wrath were still to be outpoured. She had come to this cheerful conclusion largely as a result of her own remarkable gift of precognition but she had been much encouraged to discover, after prolonged research, that her views were fully supported by such unquestioned authorities as the Prophet Ezekiel, the Great Pyramid and St. John on Patmos. This intelligence plunged her only child, a pious but perhaps over-imaginative lad, into a state of gloom bordering on panic not noticeably relieved by her cheerful assertion that all these heralded disasters were but a prelude to the Second Coming when all the redeemed—among whom, as fully paid-up members of the Lost Ten Tribes, we had a very good chance of being numbered—would be caught up out of their gross, terrestrial bodies and transferred to the Astral Plane, there to grow in wisdom and holiness throughout eternity. For although only just nine years old I had a strong feeling that my gross terrestrial body offered possibilities of enjoyment as yet unexploited and I took a rather dim, in both senses of the word, view of the Astral Plane. My childish sentiments, in fact, are best summed up by some lines written many years later in a different context.

> "For Thy coming, Lord we pray,
> But let it be some other day.
> On Thy return our hopes are set;
> Thy Will be done, but not just yet."

To what exactly my mother's life-long pursuit of Hidden Wisdom, for which she always seemed to me to be temperamentally quite unsuited, owed its origin I have never been able to decide. Was it, perhaps, a form of escapism encouraged by the conditions of her early life? On the death of her mother her father, who shortly married again, had returned to China leaving her in the care of her grandmother, a formidable old lady who had found salvation at the feet of that pillar of the Low Church, Prebendary Webb-Peploe, then Vicar of St. Paul's, Onslow Square, and who ran her household on strictly Evangelical lines which my mother may well have felt unduly restricting. Moreover, searching the scriptures for hints of things to come, preferably unpleasant, has always been a favourite pastime of extreme Protestantism and this may well have come to play a compensatory role in an otherwise not very colourful childhood.

Or did this strange preoccupation with The Beyond develop later, when my mother was in her teens, as an unconscious sublimation of rather different longings which in her day and class were quite impossible of fulfilment and of the nature of which she was quite certainly ignorant? She did once tell me that she had first become aware of her psychic powers, of which I must disloyally confess I never witnessed any very convincing manifestation, while at finishing school in Brussels where she had been much in demand for séances and table-turnings usually held, she coyly added, presumably by way of social justification, in the Japanese Legation. There can, however, be small doubt that her enthusiasm was much strengthened, and received its peculiar colouring, in the studio of G. F. Watts, then passing through his final, apocalyptic phase, whose last surviving pupil she lived to become, and was further reinforced by a close study of the Pre-Raphaelites.

In her appearance there was not, at any stage of my mother's life, any marked suggestions of otherworldliness. Very short, robust, with great width of jaw and very beautiful pale blue eyes never, in my experience, illuminated by anything approaching a mystic gleam, she habitually radiated a cheerful determination to get her own way that had led the better disposed among her relations to describe her as "very capable", others as "bossy". Sensibly, rather than smartly, dressed, the only discernible hint of the greenery-yallery which her presence afforded was occasioned by a deplorable weakness, which she never quite overcame, for artistic jewellery laboriously handwrought in what was hoped was a Celtic style by a distressed gentlewoman in Glastonbury.

After marriage my mother's psychic and artistic gifts remained for a time unparaded. Nor was this surprising as my father, a cheerful, irreverent man whose spiritual require-ments were undoubtedly fully met by Freemasonry and his duties as church-warden and whose preferred artist was Phil May, can never have provided an ideal audience for revelation. Moreover, his leisure hours were fully taken up with getting sufficient outdoor exercise, an advantage of which all Lancasters were determined not to deprive themselves or others, and to exploit which in the fullest possible measure we temporarily abandoned Kensington.

The chief, and in my mother's eyes only, merit of our new residence in Sheen was the opportunity it afforded my father for riding in Richmond Park before breakfast; an opportunity of which he had, alas, but a short time to avail himself. The house, just off Sheen Lane, was a largish, pebble-dashed and white-balconied number with a spacious garden that was yet not sufficiently so to compensate for the inconvenience of the internal arrangements. The only room of which I retain today any very clear recollection was the drawing-room which my mother, greatly daring, had decorated in a Chinese style inspired by several visits to a highly popular oriental drama called *Mr. Wu* in which her favourite actor, Mr. Matheson Lang, was currently appearing.

East Sheen was, at that date, going through an uncomfortable period of transition. Surrounded on all sides, save on that adjoining Richmond Park, by the stifling red-brick and fancy tile-work of Edwardian suburbia, the centre of the village still displayed faint traces of the rural, Rowlandsonian past. The Bull Inn had not yet been rebuilt in Brewer's neo-Georgian and not only retained its courtyard and dignified brown-brick façade, but once a week, when with much hornblowing my uncle's four-in-hand drove up for the first change of horses on the weekly run from The Berkeley to Hampton Court, fulfilled its original function. Opposite, at the bottom of Sheen Lane, there still stood an enormous chestnut in the shade of which a few old gaffers were accustomed, perhaps a trifle self-consciously, to sit on summer evenings, while Sheen Lane itself was flanked for much of its length by eighteenth-century stables and high demesne walls above which loomed the tops of gigantic cedars.

But all these vestiges of a dignified past were quite powerless to reconcile me to the odious present. Richmond Park I hated, contrasting its wide open spaces, dotted with blasted oaks and inhabited only by deer, unfavourably with the jolly social whirl of the Broad Walk with its dignified elms. It induced in me a feeling of loneliness and depression and in all the long, grey afternoons, during which I was mercilessly dragged through its far too extensive rides, the only incident I can recall with pleasure was an encounter with two ladies of, to me, fabulous elegance and distinction driving in an open victoria under

violet-tinted parasols. With rare presence of mind Nanny called me smartly to attention, for I was wearing my sailor suit, and bade me give a proper naval salute to which Queen Alexandra and the Dowager Empress of Russia gravely responded with a gracious inclination of the head.

In retrospect our period at Sheen remains inescapably identified with the gloom and misery of the First War, and whereas Kensington and the Bayswater Road are forever bathed in the perpetual sunlight of the days before 1914, over Sheen and its surroundings the clouds are low and grey and the wind blows coldly with a hint of sleet. Of the war itself I recall little enough—a captive balloon breaking away from its moorings in Richmond Park; a purple-lettered poster, seen from my pram, in the Upper Richmond Road announcing the death of Kitchener; leaning from an upstairs window to watch a daylight air-raid, hundreds of little balls of dirty cotton-wool drifting and expanding against the London sky with, way above them, barely detectable, a cloud of scattering mosquitoes. What, however, has not faded is the memory of the overall and increasing depression which, even for a child, coloured life on the home-front during that earlier conflict and which was so mercifully absent during the last. The endless casualty lists, the appalling prevalence of mourning which turned London into the magnified likeness of one of those French provincial towns which seem to be inhabited exclusively by widows, and, later, the constant hunger which neither the too frequent appearance on the nursery table of a horrible ersatz concoction known as honey-sugar, nor generous helpings of lentil-soup, seemed ever wholly to satisfy—all combined, in a way in which queues, bombings and blackout never did, to induce a permanent lowness of spirit. Perhaps the only real advantage (for a personal safety in wartime is not invariably an advantage for the civilian population) which the First War had over the Second was the absence of sirens. For the brave tooting bugles blown by boy scouts on bicycles, so far from turning the stomach over, promoted a feeling of pleasurable, if faintly comic, bravado.

On my mother the war had, at first, a distinctly bracing effect. Contemplation was abandoned for action and that side of her character which her appearance so strongly reflected found, for perhaps the only time in her life, full scope for development. For despite her transcendentalism my mother was always a New Woman at heart; in her younger days when she had moved in the intellectual circle centring round the Cobden Sanderson house on Chiswick Mall, she had been staunchly pro-Boer, a keen, although not militant, supporter of Women's Suffrage, and she always remained a dedicated Shavian. Forewarned from Beyond of the imminence of war she had, in the years immediately preceding the outbreak, taken a series of courses in First Aid and become an enthusiastic recruit to the newly formed Red Cross, so that she now found herself well equipped by experience, and still more by temperament, to raise and train a local detachment. In this great work of education, I, too, played my part, spending many a long evening on the platform in schools and church halls being bandaged and unbandaged in demonstration of the correct procedure to be adopted to meet every variety of wound and fracture. Incidentally, it was in the same cause that I made my first appearance on any stage, when, dressed in rags and representing Gallant Little Belgium, I was clasped to the protective bosom of a local Britannia in a patriotic *tableau vivant* that produced, so I have always been given to understand, a very powerful effect.

My reaction to my father's death in 1916 was one of shattering disappointment rather than overwhelming grief. He had been away for seemingly so long that, although he had always remained a cherished and deeply missed figure, his image was fast becoming legendary. It was all the more bitter, therefore, that the dreaded slip of paper should have arrived on the very day he was due back on leave and that instead of his jovial presence in the nursery restoring and revitalising my love and appreciation I should have been confronted with weeping relatives in the drawing-room. Of the following weeks I retain only a confused memory of memorial services and black-edged writing paper, of crêpe arm-bands being sewn on my jackets and overcoat, and of desperate and futile efforts to obey the constantly repeated injunction to be a comfort to my mother. She for her part, once the first shock was over, concentrated more fiercely than ever on her Red Cross activities so that I now found myself increasingly in the exclusive company of Nanny and the domestic staff which, although deeply appreciated, was not, perhaps, that best calculated to fit me for the rigours of school-life in which I was shortly to be enmeshed.

Occasionally, however, I was privileged to accompany my mother to the headquarters of the Red Cross, to which she had recently been transferred, in a large and gloomy mansion on the corner of Eaton Square. The tedium of these visits, during which I was enjoined to sit quietly with a good book while my mother got on with her work, was considerable and would have been insupportable had I not made, quite early on, an interesting discovery. Owing to some technical deficiency the overflow from the lavatory alongside my mother's office, which was on the top floor, cascaded straight into the street below, immediately opposite the front door. And by skilful manipulation of the plug this flood could be controlled and timed to coincide with the arrival of visitors. The best, and last, catch of a distinguished bag was Lady Northcliffe, an imposing figure in magnificent sables, who provoked investigation by commenting in some bewilderment

on the sudden downpour from a cloudless sky which had drenched her on alighting from her car, an unnatural phenomenon which marked the end of my visits to Eaton Square.

With the coming of peace my mother's first action was to shake the dust of Sheen off her feet and move straight back to Bayswater. St. Petersburg Place, where she purchased a recently erected terrace house in the neo-Georgian style, was, and indeed still is, a short street off the Bayswater Road better endowed ecclesiastically than any other street of its length in London. At one end towers the West End Synagogue, twin-turreted in vaguely oriental red brick, at the other stands the Greek Orthodox Cathedral, conventionally if unconvincingly Byzantine, and in the middle St. Matthew's (C. of E.) raises to Heaven a lofty and uncompromisingly Evangelical spire; while just around the corner in the Queen's Road is, or was, the Ethical Church, the only place of worship in London adorned with a stained-glass window of George Bernard Shaw.

However, none of these fanes save, occasionally on wet days, St. Matthew's, which was normally too bleakly Low even for one brought up in the shadow of St. Paul's, Onslow Square, received my mother's patronage. On Sunday mornings she resumed attendance at St. John's, Notting Hill, from which, alas, much of the pre-war glory had departed (not a frock-coat in sight and only Sir Aston Webb still sporting a top-hat), but in the afternoons made pilgrimage to far less orthodox shrines propagating an extraordinary variety of esoteric doctrines.

The years immediately following the First War witnessed the emergence in London of a whole host of thaumaturges and mystagogues both lay and clerical, and of the latter there can have been few at whose feet my mother did not at one time or another sit. As I grew older my unenthusiastic presence beside her was more frequently insisted on, but of all these innumerable Magi I retain clear recollections of only one or two. There was the Reverend Fearon who had at one time been curate to Archdeacon Wilberforce, a prelate for whom my mother always retained a peculiar reverence, and who presided over the destinies of the Church Mystical Union in a particularly depressing brick church in Norfolk Square wearing a scarlet cassock and a short, blond bob. In his sermons, which were long and largely incomprehensible, the word "anthropomorphic" used exclusively in a pejorative sense was of frequent occurrence, and the ritual was marked by long, long pauses of total silence during which we were exhorted to empty our minds of all extraneous thoughts and concentrate on Perfect Oneness. Try as I would, despite clouds of encouraging incense, the successful accomplishment of this feat always eluded me and, long before I came within spitting distance of Perfect Oneness, extraneous thoughts came crowding back, most of them lubricious.

After my mother finally broke with the Church Mystical Union, for reasons which I have long since forgotten, there followed a period spiritually dominated by a portly faith-healer who was also, I think, a lay-preacher whose services, to which mercifully I was only infrequently taken, consisted, as far as I can remember, almost entirely of silent prayer. Of his successor, however, the Bishop of Basil Street, my memories are vivid. This ecclesiastical ham whose charlatanism was, even for a schoolboy, palpable, claimed to have been consecrated by the Old Catholic Archbishop of Utrecht and wore the conventional purple-piped soutane and skull cap of a Roman bishop. His cathedral, known, if I remember rightly, as The Sanctuary, a Jacobean-style hall tucked away behind Harrods, was furnished, along with more familiar *bondieuseries*, with statues of Buddha, Zoroaster and Pythagoras, and boasted in addition a lavishly gilded bishop's throne in Wardour-Street

Gothic which had once belonged, so the Bishop claimed, to Sarah Bernhardt. The congregation, numerous and well-heeled, was largely feminine but included one or two prominent merchant bankers whose credulity, so naïvely exalted was my childish estimate of Lombard Street shrewdness, never ceased to astonish me; the services were liturgically elaborate but despite the Bishop's wide experience and carefree borrowings there always clung to them a faint suggestion of improvisation inducing an embarrassment which at length outweighed the fascinated curiosity which first acquaintance had aroused. On the whole, therefore, it was a great relief when my mother finally abandoned The Sanctuary and joined a Lodge of female Freemasons from attendance at whose rites my sex debarred me.

That my mother escaped the besotted absorption, and inevitable exploitation, to which so many of the richer female members of such congregations fall victim, was due to an unusual combination of qualities. All her life she retained a robust sense of humour and a curious ability to achieve, suddenly and without warning, an almost cynical detachment when the spectacle of others' credulity would provoke her to hoots of happy laughter. Moreover she was safeguarded financially both by a recurrent, although fortunately erroneous, conviction that she was as poor as a church mouse and also by a strong feeling that there was safety in numbers. Never at any moment did any one creed command her exclusive allegiance, and to the variety of movements and organisations with which she maintained contact the periodical literature that accumulated in the Chinese drawing-room (her first exercise in oriental decoration had been repeated on a more lavish scale in St. Petersburg Place) bore abundant testimony.

There was the *Occult Review*, displaying on its orange cover a wide selection of cabalistic signs and symbols, of which the contents were usually improbable but only occasionally fascinating; tall stories of reincarnation alternated with articles on ectoplasm and long accounts of Tibetan wonder-workers. Altogether classier and better produced, rather in the style of the *Burlington Magazine*, was the *Rosy Cross*, the official organ of the Rosicrucians. This was largely devoted to the exposition of the teachings of Rudolf Steiner but published from time to time fascinating photographs of the extraordinary buildings, in a style midway between Erich Mendelsohn and Arthur Rackham, which were being erected at the cult's headquarters in Weimar. And once, curiously enough, there appeared an article by Arthur Symons on Toulouse-Lautrec, not one would have thought the most other-worldly of artists, which first fired my enthusiasm for that painter's work. To the *Theosophists' Monthly*, packed with hot tips from the Krishnamurti stable and fighting leaders from Mrs. Besant, my mother's devotion was short-lived, her subscription being promptly cancelled after hearing a thing or two about the private life of Dr. Leadbeater.

But of all the innumerable periodicals from which she from time to time derived comfort and instruction that to which my mother remained the most abidingly loyal, maintaining her readership up to the day of her death, was the *National Message and Banner*, the official publication of the British Israelites. In outward appearance there was little, save the crossed flags of Britain and the United States reproduced in colour on the cover, to distinguish it from the average parish magazine; but the contents, although often fraught with menace, reducing me in my younger days to a pitiful state of terror and apprehension, were irresistible. There were learned articles demonstrating that the circumference of the inner circle at Stonehenge if measured in cubits was exactly equal to the height of the pillars in King Solomon's temple multiplied by twelve (a number of portentous significance); there were closely reasoned arguments, which even as a child I judged slightly specious, showing that the popularity and antiquity of "Danny Boy" provided powerful support for the theory that the Irish were, in fact, of the tribe of Dan. Nor were current affairs neglected, always being approached from a strictly Conservative angle and usually interpreted in the light of that certain knowledge which a close study of the Great Pyramid alone afforded. Indeed it was these editorial comments which most frequently sent me shivering to bed and coloured my dreams when I got there. For no matter how cheerful the news nor how quiet the international situation, the wrath to come, here on earth, was inescapable and getting very close now. The fact that the English-speaking peoples, provided that they did not go whoring after strange gods such as the League of Nations and never adopted the decimal system, would, thanks to the promises given to their forefather Abraham, emerge triumphant in the end, did little to reassure me; the length and nature of the tribulations which would have first to be undergone suggested too low a rating for my personal chances of survival. That the plan and dimensions of the Great Pyramid, or rather their interpretation, provided on occasion less than completely accurate information on the shape of things to come was small comfort. If some particular date to be marked by irreparable disaster passed without incident this was invariably attributed to some marginal error in the measurement of the Passage to the Tomb-chamber and the load of woe transferred a few years ahead. Only when they were retrospective could I regard such re-adjustments with equanimity, as when the year 1923, which had long been forecast as the beginning of the end, having drawn to its close unmarked by any very spectacular calamity, it was discovered that the sinister crack at that particular point in the Passage was clear reference to our resumption of the Gold Standard. A lamentable decision, doubtless, and one with far-reaching consequences, but which left me as a schoolboy comparatively unmoved.

One strange feature of this astonishing publication which puzzled me at the time, but which subsequent experience has led me to regard as generally indicative, was the high proportion of naval officers, both active and retired, among the contributors. Why is it, I wonder, that no cause, from Homœopathy to Fascism, is so dotty that it cannot attract loyal support from at least one Rear Admiral (Retd.) or Captain, R.N.?

My mother's studies were not, however, confined exclusively to periodical literature; our bookcases groaned beneath the weight of innumerable volumes with such titles as *Behind the Beyond* or *The Yogi Way*. Fortunately for me, a child much given to browsing, this esoteric flood never completely overwhelmed the shelves reserved for Thackeray and Kipling, nor those which reflected my father's taste on which both Saki and W. W. Jacobs were well represented. But as time went on books tended increasingly to stray from appointed sections and I shall never forget my surprise and delight when one day I discovered, tucked away between *In Tune with the Infinite* and the poems of Rabindranath Tagore, *More Gals' Gossip* by Arthur Binstead of *The Pink 'Un*, discreetly jacketed in plain brown paper.

How carefully, in fact, my mother studied all the massive tomes which she acquired in ever-increasing numbers I was never wholly certain. On more than one occasion, having departed to bed with the *Bhagavad Gita* or *The Cloud of Unknowing* prominently displayed beneath her arm, I subsequently discovered her, when I went to say good-night, deep in the latest work of Miss Ethel M. Dell. Always on such occasions her response, uttered in a very reproachful tone, to any expression of surprise was the same, "You know quite well, dear, that the bent bow must be unstrung."

Fortunately for me my mother never found any difficulty in pursuing her less specialised interests, among which the theatre ranked high. This was in a way curious as in the evangelical surroundings of her childhood the playhouse was anathema. But fortunately her grandmother had, before her own salvation, been a devoted playgoer with a marked preference for opera and ballet (I still possess an ivory model of Vestris' leg which the old lady used as a seal) and seldom tired of recalling for the benefit of her grand-daughter the exact nature of the temptations to which the fortunate child would never be exposed. But if she had long outgrown these early prohibitions, my mother always retained a slightly puritanical attitude towards playgoing that was reinforced rather than diminished by her Shavian loyalties. Thus musical comedies and revues were regarded with marked disfavour as being certainly trivial and probably immoral. Exception was made in favour of *Chu Chin Chow* on account of its oriental setting, and, curiously enough, the music hall which, although she herself never displayed much enthusiasm for red-nosed comedians, she held to be justified, in so far as I was concerned, by my father's preference for that form of entertainment. And it is entirely thanks to her unselfish attitude that I can now recall such figures as Alfred Lester, George Robey and Harry Tate in their heyday, a privilege for which I remain eternally grateful.

Mysticism, luckily for me, did not make much impact on the theatre of the twenties but whenever it did my mother was right out there on the touch-line and it is on record that she attended no less than twenty-two performances of *The Immortal Hour*. On one occasion in Paris, having been informed by an American spiritualist painter of her acquaintance that a Hindu dancer, whose performance was fraught with mystic significance, was currently appearing at the Casino de Paris, I was taken to a revue called *Paris en fleurs* in which, rather to her surprise but not, I think, altogether to her regret, the other performers included Maurice Chevalier and the Dolly Sisters, and which was from time to time enlivened by dance-routines that were not remotely tinged with mysticism.

While opera, apart from *The Immortal Hour*, had little or no appeal for my mother, although out of respect for my father, an ardent Wagnerian, she always referred to *The Ring* in a very reverential way, she had inherited to the full her grandmother's passion for the ballet and it was to this that I owed the first great aesthetic experience of my childhood.

The ease and completeness with which so many people seem able to recall over a lapse of many years every roulade and entrechat of some historic production arouses in me a doubtless unjustified scepticism. Certainly any such feat of total recall is quite beyond my powers; and of the 1919 Diaghilev production of *The Sleeping Beauty* almost all that I can now remember is Lopokova as the Lilac Fairy, the dazzling beauty of the Bakst sets and the intensity of my own response. Nothing I had ever seen had in any way prepared me for the magnificence that was disclosed on the rise of the curtain of The Alhambra, and for weeks afterwards my drawing books were packed with hopeful but pathetic attempts to recapture something of the glory of that matinée, and there and then I formed an ambition that was not destined to be fulfilled for more than thirty years.

While nothing else in my theatrical experience as a child ever achieved so great an impact, several notable performances still remain vivid: Mr. Henry Ainley as Mark Antony; Mr. Miles Malleson as Lancelot Gobbo in a production at The Court Theatre in which the great Jewish actor Moritz Moskowitz won universal praise for his interpretation of Shylock, a performance of which I remember not one single line nor gesture; a quite unknown young actor called Coward in *The Knight of the Burning Pestle*; Miss Dorothy Green as Lady Macbeth in the dear old half-timbered theatre at Stratford and, needless to say, Mr. Matheson Lang playing Matheson Lang in a whole series of cloak-and-dagger dramatisations of novels by Rafael Sabatini, an author for whose work I had the keenest admiration. Occasionally these memories are not wholly of enjoyment; of *St. Joan* what I now most clearly recall is my resentment of the *faux-naif*, breathless tone of voice, suggesting a particularly maddening girl-guide at a rather difficult stage in her development, which Dame Sybil saw fit to maintain throughout, that almost outweighed my excited appreciation of the play itself and of the outstanding beauty of the costumes designed by Charles Ricketts.

While my mother's determination to keep abreast of all that was worthiest in modern culture remained constant she could never bring herself, anyhow when I was young, to include the cinema as coming under that heading. It was, in her view, invariably an undesirably sensational form of entertainment that always took place in the most unhygienic surroundings, and the grave risk of "catching things" reduced my visits to a minimum. Almost the only exception was made in favour of the Polytechnic in Regent Street, whether because the connection with Quintin Hogg was considered to have a sterilising effect, or because the film of Scott's expedition to the Antarctic had first been shown there, I never knew. Personally, I always felt this ban to be monstrously unfair, the more particularly as it did not apply to my little cousins who never missed an episode of *The Perils of Pauline*, and I can still recapture the pangs of frustrated longing aroused by the sight of the powerfully conceived posters for *The Birth of a Nation*. In later life, however, my mother's attitude was somewhat relaxed and, accompanied by her devoted maid, she was accustomed to make regular weekly excursions to her local. But she always remained a trifle ashamed of these dissipations and her reaction when taxed was the same as that aroused by any adverse comment on her devotion to the works of Ethel M. Dell.

One reason, I fancy, why my mother never wholly surmounted her guilt feelings about the cinema lay in the fact that it was so frequently preoccupied with sex, a subject which she found not so much distasteful as virtually incomprehensible. With her, as with so many well-educated women of that generation, emancipation was conditioned by background and, while she never wavered in her conviction that men and women were equally entitled to the same freedom, she never for one moment doubted, in so far as pre- or extra-marital experience was concerned, that this was best achieved by restricting the male rather than by any extension of indulgence to the female. Nothing infuriated her more than to hear any light-hearted reference to the sowing of wild oats. Deeply as she had loved my father, physical passion, I am convinced, in her case played but a small part in their relationship: a view in which I was confirmed many years later when on the eve of my own wedding she took the bride aside for a little good advice. "Now, dear, I want you to promise me that you won't let Osbert be tiresome. I know what those Lancasters are like when given half a chance and I was always very firm with his dear father."

Towards less orthodox manifestations of the sexual urge she displayed an engaging tolerance founded on total ignorance. Among her numerous artistic acquaintances there were several djibbah-clad couples whose mutual affection would, to a more sophisticated eye, have seemed long since to have passed the normal bounds of feminine friendship but in whose relationship my mother saw nothing remotely equivocal. And once, when staying with friends in France where a distinguished writer was a fellow-guest, she wrote me, "There is a Monsieur Gide staying here at present. I must say I find him very courteous but they tell me he is a little like Oscar Wilde—you know what I mean, dear." I did but remained doubtful whether the knowledge was shared.

To the art of painting my mother's attitude was enthusiastic but confused. Well-trained, first

in Brussels, then in Watts' studio and subsequently, round the turn of the century, at St. Ives, her practice (for immediately on our return to London she rented a studio) remained strictly orthodox; but the fact that she continued, year after year, to exhibit well-painted but conventional flower-pieces at the Royal Academy in no way inhibited her appreciation of those more experimental works for which she had first conceived an enthusiasm at the historic Grosvenor Galleries exhibition in 1912. Unfortunately her admiration did not go so far as to lead her to purchase any examples; on the very few occasions when she brought out her cheque-book it was almost always for the acquisition of some opalescent watercolour in which ill-defined forms loomed through violet clouds, painted, it was claimed, under the direct control of a spirit-guide. This was in a way curious as the nearest she herself got to mysticism in her own work was the occasional introduction of a wooden statuette of Buddha into a solidly conceived still-life. Nevertheless, if she neglected many a golden opportunity (either from recurrent fears of imminent financial disaster or from a well-justified apprehension of the alarming reaction which the patronage of contemporary art would undoubtedly provoke in her in-laws), her approach always remained, to my infinite advantage, professional and catholic, and from a very early age I was not only encouraged in my own efforts but was her regular companion at private views at the Leicester Galleries and the winter exhibitions at Burlington House. Indeed, it was to this determination that I should enjoy as wide and as early an acquaintance as possible with the work of the Masters both in painting and architecture that finally led her to overcome her reluctance to venture on the post-war continent without adult male protection.

"He says he's a Lt.-Col. Fanshawe, and thinks there must have been a muddle about the tickets."

morning for Assiut. American style car. v
...e to eat one's lunch. Arrived at Assiut about
...at large. v. comfortable in good old-fashioned
..., black lacquer and gold. Alan and Lucy's in
...istrate. Also aboard the Blisses and party
...graceful. Palms, intense cultivation, odd
...ast sometimes right on the horizon, at
...wider than I had thought. Very open but
has some turbaned figure doing something
most elaborate buildings the dovecotes.

AN ENGLISHMAN ABROAD

His work makes it plain that Osbert Lancaster had a well developed appetite for travel. A modicum of discomfort was acceptable provided the sights were sufficiently interesting, but was not embraced for its own sake, as with so many professional globetrotters. Osbert's writings and drawings, particularly the former, make it equally clear that he never identified with 'abroad', as at every moment he remained conscious of being an Englishman. His first love among foreign countries was undoubtedly Greece. Despite the fact that his first book about Greece was entitled *Classical Landscape With Figures*, it seems to have been the 'unclassical' aspects of the Greek character which he relished most deeply—the intransigent individualism he saw everywhere about him. *Sailing to Byzantium*, a more scholarly enterprise, demonstrates Osbert's ability to vivify an apparently dry and technical subject. He successfully straddles two genres which are often antipathetic to one another—pure travel writing and architectural history.

ITALIAN AFTERNOON

I N YONDER marble hero's shade
Aunt Drusilla used to sit
With her memories of the Slade
And her water-colour kit.

There, E. V. Lucas lay, well-thumbed, beside her,
Buckling a little in the foreign sun,
While round that dim *Risorgimento* rider
[Claiming some long-forgotten vict'ry won]
The circling pigeons' flight grew ever wider,
Fainter the echoes of the midday gun.

Across the square a monsignore
Late for his siesta goes:
The prison scene from *Trovatore*
Dies on a dozen radios.

FROM AN ITALIAN SKETCHBOOK

Article written for *The World Off Duty,* 1947

Osbert Lancaster revisits the scene where the Eighth Army made their last spectacular advance. There are still many relics of war in the plain between Venice and Padua, but the bridges and campaniles are rising again from their ruins, and the lush vegetation is masking the burns and scars of the battlefields.

THE hill on which stands the village of Asolo is the first Alpine ridge to break the surface of the plain north-east of Venice. From its walls the view extends, on a clear day, from the lagoons on the coast to the slight swell in the ground behind which lie the towers and palaces of Vicenza; between these two limits stretches the vast indigo arc of the plain, bounded in the south by the horizon and far, far flatter than your hand. Here and there above the dark green carpet of vegetation rise up slender campaniles marking the whereabouts of the innumerable towns and villages—Treviso, six thousand of whose inhabitants were, thanks to the superlative accuracy of modern bomb-sights, wiped out in five minutes, Castelfranco, the birthplace of Giorgione, and, right away on the horizon, Padua, the oldest university city in Europe and now British GHQ.

There can be few vantage points in the world from which it is possible to see at one time so extensive a tract of a country in which so much of first-rate importance in the history of the human race has occurred. This great plain, fading away into the haze, that lies between the Alps and the Appenines and is bisected by the Po, immensely fertile and carefully cultivated since the dawn of history, has been the never-failing magnet that has drawn race after race down from the mountain passes to the north and, as a result, acted as a forcing ground for new cultures. Venice, just visible beyond the industrial smudge of Mestre, was for centuries the only channel beween the Greek and Syrian East and the

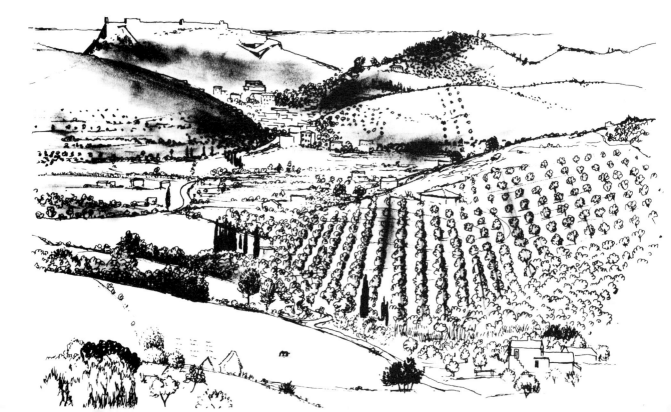

Latin West, and beyond it to the south lies Ravenna, hidden in the sea haze, which, during the terrible fifth century of our era, maintained a clear civilised glow amidst the barbarian gloom. Later, all these little cities and towns marked some step in the progress of recovery; Modena, where are still preserved the earliest examples of the first school of European sculpture that arose after the classical collapse; Ferrara, the first city to be laid out to a scientific town plan; Vicenza, the birthplace of Palladio, who was so surprisingly and permanently to affect the whole course of English architecture. One by one these thriving centres, existing precariously between the rival great powers of Venice and Milan, lost their independence; in time their captors were themselves led captive, first by Napoleon, then by Austria, and finally by the Kingdom of united Italy.

Today, thanks largely to the aftermath of war, the centralising tendency of the previous centuries seems for the first time to have gone into reverse. With bridges destroyed, rolling stock vanished no one knows where, and petrol scarce, communications operate at an almost medieval tempo. During the long night of occupation, hostages and partisans, law and order lost much of their old accepted power and the foothills are still full of robbers. Down the long roads trail a sinister collection of "displaced persons", Yugoslavs, Poles, Jews, British and American deserters, all desperate and many armed. No one in their senses goes far afield after dark. The Central Government is far away and almost universally regarded as a bad joke, the currency inspires no confidence, and land, good fertile acres, is the only dependable capital. It is not, in these circumstances, surprising that the small town should once more have resumed its old independent role; its market, operating frequently enough by barter, completely overshadows for the local merchants and financiers the bourses of Milan and Rome; its mayor, controlling the local bus service and police, has become a far more acceptable source of authority than the Ministries of Transport and Security in the capital; and the local landlords, farmers and peasants are infinitely more influential figures than the unfortunate bureaucracy who for a starvation wage pretend to carry out the usually incomprehensible orders and directives of a despised Government.

At a time when we are being assured by all the experts that our only hope lies in global planning, that small units are administratively incompetent and economically doomed, this tendency is likely to receive little encouragement and will appear to many to be the first indication of a coming lapse into barbarism. This is not a view I can wholeheartedly share. When one sees the amount of reconstruction which has been carried out in this plain, where the destruction was far more extensive than I personally, and I suspect many others, had ever realised—a new bridge here, a campanile rebuilt there, new barns and cottages everywhere—and when one realises that the majority of these works have been accomplished entirely by local talent, unassisted and unadvised by any Ministry of Town and Country Planning and unfinanced by any reconstruction loan, one's faith in the apostles of centralisation at all costs is more than a little shaken. In particular, one is struck and encouraged by the fact that here, unlike our own country, cultural monuments receive a priority: the nave of the great church of San Francesco in Bologna has been almost completely rebuilt, the apse of San Ambrogio at Milan entirely restored, and everywhere damage to churches and palaces is being made good. If local pride can achieve so much, if so high a standard of values can prevail in localities upon which a new independence and isolation have been forced by external events, it would seem to indicate that parochialism may not, after all, be so justified a term of reproach as we have latterly come so unreflectingly to imagine.

55

FRENCH AFTERNOON

I SHALL not linger in that draughty square
Attracted by the art-nouveau hotel
Nor ring in vain the concierge's bell
And then, engulfed by a profound despair
That finds its echo in the passing trains,
Sit drinking in the café, wondering why,
Maddened by love, a butcher at Versailles
On Tuesday evening made to jump his brains.
Nor shall I visit the Flamboyant church,
Three stars in Michelin, yet by some strange fluke
Left unrestored by Viollet-le-Duc,
To carry out some long-desired research.
Too well I know the power to get one down
Exerted by this grey and shuttered town.

Osbert had a keen appreciation of the French way of life, as his autobiographical writings reveal. Clearly, however, he preferred the vernacular aspects of French architecture to grander buildings such as the Hôtel des Invalides, Chenonceaux or Chartres, which do not appear in his drawings.

GREECE

Osbert's love of Greece and the Greeks was very much that of a new generation of Hellenists. Byzantium interested him more than Periclean Athens, and he became a great authority on Byzantine architecture. But he refused to concentrate exclusively on the past. The contemporary inhabitants of Greece are portrayed in his writing, and in his drawings, with immense affection and amusement.

Reproduced below, this page from one of Osbert's Greek sketchbooks shows the elegance of his handwriting and the complete integration of picture and text which characterises these volumes.

BACK to KHANIA   Further exploration revealed quite a lot of remains of the Venetian fortifications plus the charming Palladian façade of the church of San Rocco, decaying gracefully altho' scheduled as historical monument. The church of San Francesco, now the museum, on the other hand, hopelessly over-restored. Typical wide-aisled Franciscan church with good vaulting. Façade hideous with artificial stone. J. took me into a private house, once a church then a mosque, with pointed barrel vaults and, in the principal room, cutting across a corner, an elaborate mihrab, I took to be 18th century, with a lot of good incised and moulded decoration and traces of colour. J also showed me a small chapel opposite his house, I should say trecento, with pointed vaults on ribs, well preserved sedilia and piscina, with the present door cut thro' what was originally the E end, and W. end blocked up. Also, in another part of the town, a very odd doorway in a very individual version of High Renaissance — combined with one or two strangely Gothic features. Presumably carried out by local talent from some Italian engraving or not wholly understood design. (See drawing)

UNLOADING AT RETHYMO

PLATANEIA   Pleasant enough little seaside village between the main-road and the sea, with, inland, the old village high on a hill. Minute half-cottage set in tamarisk grove fifty yards from water's edge. Long sandy beach with a ruined mill in it

AEGEAN
AFTERNOON

BENEATH the kite-encumbered sky
There reigns a silence in the heat
Which natives here would classify
As tense, unbroken and complete.
An Asia Minor refugee
Wails a nostalgic Turkish song.
The priest at the Asomatoi
Is beating on a wooden gong
And fishermen far out at sea
Are dynamiting all day long.
In the spongeshop Vassilias
Gives a deep, responsive snore
As the steamer from Piraeus,
Hooting loudly, nears the shore.

INTRODUCTION
Taken from *Classical Landscape with Figures,* 1947

FEW branches of literature have been so diligently cultivated in the last few years as that dealing with foreign countries and, as intense activity invariably results in change of form, the old-fashioned travel book has become a thing of the past. Gone are those fat green volumes with wide margins, thinly spaced type and, by way of frontispiece, a sepia photograph, slightly out of focus, of the authoress on her favourite mule contemplating through bewildered pince-nez the ruins of Baalbek. The Wanderers and the Ramblers with their Watman sketching-pads and HB pencils and limited but genuine culture have been replaced by the socially conscious reporter and the witty introvert. This being the case, it is only honest to point out by way of warning to the resolutely contemporary that, lacking both the self-confidence and keen social conscience necessary for inclusion in the latter school, I approximate spiritually more to the mule-riding female watercolourist, and that the present work is likely to be considered closer in feeling to *Little Walks in Leafy Umbria* (now unfortunately out of print) than to *Storm in the Caucasus* or *Wings over Olympus.* Having issued this warning I can freely point out that my aim has been slightly different from those of any of the above and considerably more old-fashioned. This is not a ramble, nor a travel book, nor yet a guide, but a *description* in the eighteenth-century meaning of the term.

It may well be pointed out that the need for an informative work of this kind dealing with Greece has long since been satisfied and that the author's energies would have been better employed in describing the Gran Chaco or even the lesser explored regions of West Kensington. But such an objection, I submit, is not so easily sustained as might be imagined for, owing to the unique position that Greece occupies in world-history, specialisation has from the first been encouraged at the expense of the general view. As a result, in modern times, anyhow since the days of the ever-admirable Colonel Leake, the literary travellers who pass across the Greek landscape tend to divide themselves into tight little groups of varying size closely following certain well-defined routes. Looming large in the foreground is a long subfusc procession of sixth-form masters and dons (the figure of the great Mahaffey leading the adolescent Oscar by the hand well to the fore) gripping tight their Pausanias and resolutely turning their backs on anything post-dating the battle of Chaeronea. Beyond are to be observed a few angry and aggressive little figures, quarrelling violently among themselves and on the worst possible terms with the classical party down below, following the dynamic form of Robert Byron bearing a banner with a strange device on which is inscribed the single word "Byzantium". More recently a new contingent has arrived, easily to be distinguished from the others by the erratic and seemingly purposeless nature of their course and by the fact that they are entirely unencumbered by guide-books or intellectual impedimenta of any sort; these display no interest in either the landscape or the ruins and close observation will show that their dartings back and forth are occasioned by the necessity under which they labour of having to put in long-distance calls to Fleet Street or New York at regular intervals.

The object of the present work, therefore, is to provide some general account of the present appearance and condition of Greece that may perhaps prove of use to that small minority who are likely in future to receive the necessary passports, visas, priorities, travel-permits and foreign exchange enabling them to leave these shores, to awaken a not-too-painful nostalgia in those who have visited the country in the past, and to provide some slight entertainment and instruction to the vast majority who lack the memories of the latter and entertain no hopes of immediate inclusion in the narrow ranks of the former. (Needless to say, this avowed intention, like so many purposes boldly proclaimed on title-pages, was, of course, only formulated when the book was nearing completion and will be taken by the wise as being in the nature of the official declaration at the customs which leaves a quantity of less disinterested and more personal motives tucked away undeclared at the bottom of the suitcase.) Having made this avowal, however, it would be both rash and improper not at once to qualify it.

The landscape which I have attempted to unroll in the following pages, though entirely Greek, is by no means the whole of Greece. Lacking the creative imagination of certain writers that enables them vividly to describe scenes and monuments which they have only beheld with the eye of faith, I have been forced to confine myself to things seen. Thus, whatever completeness was intended, the result is at once observed to be marred by a number of large blanks, many occurring in irritatingly important parts of the canvas, and not even the dim lines of a preliminary sketch are visible in the places which should properly be occupied by Macedonia, Thrace, most of Thessaly, the Cyclades and the south-western corner of the Peloponnese. Less important but still sufficiently annoying in a landscape that is avowedly topographical, are further sections which should by rights be richly detailed but which have in fact been lightly indicated in an unavoidably impressionist technique. To these faults of omission must be added others that arise from undue emphasis: the lighting will be found to be sadly uneven in its distribution, frequently illuminating the architecture with a distracting brilliance while leaving the flora and fauna in almost impenetrable gloom and imparting a chiaroscuro from which the Byzantine cupola emerges more frequently than the classical colonnade.

These grave inadequacies I readily acknowledge and regret, but to a further criticism which may well be levelled I have a reply. It may be contended that in a work intended to give a picture of the Greek scene as it presents itself today so obvious a preoccupation with the past is entirely misplaced; or conversely, that in a landscape which at the present time can only be regarded as historic such contemporary elements as intrude are as uncalled for and as irritating as the little boy in the cloth cap who invariably slips into the foreground of what would otherwise have been an exquisite camera study of the ruins of Sunion or the bay of Salamis. But the present and the past are always and everywhere inseparable; scratch is a position from which one can never start, and history a meaningless fantasy if not interpreted in the light of present-day experience. In Greece, where a more determined effort to disregard it has been made than almost anywhere else on earth, this truth is more than usually inescapable. Here, where it is still too often assumed that nothing of importance ever happened between the death of Alexander and the arrival of Byron and that, as a result of this long interregnum, all threads connecting antiquity with the present day had long since perished or been broken, every other mile affords vivid demonstration of an intimate inter-penetration of epochs. The pillars of the Ionic temple are found built into the fabric of the Byzantine monastery, the Cyclopean masonry of the Mycenean strong point has been re-erected to protect an Axis gun-site and the mortar batteries of ELAS have left scars on the Acropolis that are already indistinguishable from those caused by Turkish gunners. In the realm of ideas this persistence of the past is no less real, though perhaps less immediately apparent; disquieting memories of the wide empire of Justinian are said occasionally to have troubled the realistic mind of Venizelos and remain uncomfortably but excitingly vivid for many of his compatriots to this day; Papandreou denounces Marshal Tito with the same lack of restraint and much of the eloquence of Demosthenes anathematising Philip of Macedon; and the Centaurs still haunt the imagination and frighten the children of the peasants of Pelion.

But by what right, it may be argued, does a landscapist concern himself with humanity at all? The presence of a picturesque peasant tastefully disposed on a broken column in the middle distance is perhaps allowable, but why is the whole foreground cluttered up with a heterogeneous collection of human oddities whose generally unromantic aspect fits them only for appearance in a newsreel? The answer is that in Greece the inhabitants are part of the landscape and that were they omitted the picture would take on an unreal lunar bareness carrying no conviction to those acquainted with the reality. For as the physical features of a country everywhere condition the character and development of the inhabitants, so in Greece the latter react in some mysterious and not easily definable way upon their surroundings, and although one may remain at a loss for a reasonable explanation one knows quite certainly that without their presence these coasts and mountains would remain as boring and as unsustaining as the Riviera or the Bernese Oberland. It is largely, of course, a matter of scale; in the high Alps or on the vast plains of eastern Europe man is reduced to complete unimportance and neither his presence nor his absence can possibly affect in the smallest degree the scene's significance, but here all the natural features seem to have been deliberately conceived in relation to our human stature. Unpeopled, these plains and valleys, headlands and coves would be as incomplete and purposeless as brilliantly illuminated settings on an empty stage. That the earliest religion of the people of this countryside should have been anthropomorphic was as inevitable as that the Egyptians should have bowed down to vultures and jackals, and the birth of humanism could only have occurred in a setting where man's proportion was so exquisitely adjusted to his environment. In the north his vision was clouded by mists and twilight and oppressed by the immensity of ocean and mountain, while in the south the featureless desert and tractable Nile exaggerated his stature and induced profitless illusions of megalomaniac grandeur.

Having thus justified my inclusion of the human element, I must straightway reveal the limited nature of my qualifications as a figure-painter. The total period of my residence in the country did not exceed eighteen months; I never succeeded in acquiring a knowledge of the language that enabled me to do more than reveal, in exceptionally favourable circumstances, the simplest of human needs; and my contacts were almost entirely confined to Athenian politicians and officials. Moreover, I am constantly humiliated by the painfully acquired knowledge that I am singularly lacking in that gift, which, to judge from their writings, is widely distributed among my contemporaries, of straightway establishing the most intimate and cordial relations with the common man of every nationality. Fortunately in Greece, where a proper degree of social consciousness remains to be enforced, this disgraceful failing is of less importance than elsewhere, for it is the common man who here at once takes the initiative and whose exquisite courtesy and insatiable curiosity easily enable him to surmount all barriers of race and language save that which, in certain rare cases, has been erected by an orthodox Marxian training.

Not only am I thus palpably ill equipped for the task I have attempted, but I have consciously added to my offence by deliberately flouting the best traditional advice. No warning is so frequently voiced to those about to write of foreign peoples as the injunction to avoid at all costs judging one's subjects by British standards. My reaction to this hoary maxim is to ask by what conceivable standard is one then to judge them. Their own? Then a lifetime spent in the country were surely insufficient to achieve the necessary qualifications. By those which it is hoped will prevail in the ideal supra-national world state of tomorrow? In that case I am too sadly out of tune with the cosmic consciousness to utter a word. Rejecting all such foolishness, insofar as I employ the comparative method, my criteria, political, architectural and scenic, remain firmly Anglo-Saxon, and the standards of judgement are always those of an Anglican graduate of Oxford with a taste for architecture, turned cartoonist, approaching middle age and living in Kensington.

Such are the standards I have unashamedly adopted; their application it will soon be discovered is almost exclusively visual. No analysis of deep underlying causes has been attempted, and no effort has been made to display an acute psychological insight. For one reason I lack both the temperament and knowledge necessary for such an enterprise; for another, I have a very shrewd suspicion that in Greece there are no deep underlying causes and that the facts which meet the eye are all-important. The Greeks are of all people the least inhibited (it is significant that the only two professional psychoanalysts practising in Athens have large private incomes) and their passions, both amorous and political, are seldom indulged under a bushel. But whereas elsewhere politics may do little to enrich the landscape, here they find visible expression in a variety of ways all of which lend character to the scene and which to omit would be to falsify the whole. Among these the red and blue slogans that form such significant patterns on the walls of every town, the banner-waving processions that every Sunday troop off to the Stadium or Syntagma are the most immediately apparent and least violent. But on occasions politics provide a more macabre emphasis to the view and indeed the first Greek figure on whom I set eyes was a bearded warrior rolling in agony in the foreground of the long perspective of an empty Kolonaki street, closed in the distance by the dramatic silhouette of Lycabettus, who had, so subsequent investigation revealed, just been slugged through the stomach by a political opponent concealed behind some shuttered second-empire façade away in the wings.

Having thus made my formal declaration at the *douane* there remain two unavowed motives which, safely across the frontier, I can now perhaps without danger confess. First, the presumptuous idea that as a great deal of nonsense, most of it ill-informed and much of it wilfully prejudiced, has recently been written about Greece, a fresh attempt to provide a picture, even one so personal and specialised as this, of a country with which, as the latest development of American foreign policy has forcefully demonstrated, our own future is so intimately bound up, might not be untimely. Second, the memory of the intense pleasure which I experienced in Greece, the significance which for me its monuments and landscape will always possess and my deep appreciation of the kindness, sympathy and spirit of the inhabitants have all combined to encourage me to some open ac-knowledgement.

THE GREEK FONDNESS FOR NOISE

Taken from *Classical Landscape with Figures,* 1947

OVERWHELMING as is the prevailing enthusiasm for politics, it is likely that the visitor to Athens will be struck more immediately by the Greek passion for noise. There are some who hold that this extraordinary trait in the national character springs rather from insensitiveness or indifference than from any positive liking; but this is a theory which I consider has been rendered untenable by my chance discovery, in a car-park in the Piraeus, of a motor-bicycle fitted with two exhausts, each provided not with a silencer but an amplifier. The means whereby this passion is given expression are manifold and ingenious and there is no department of life in which it is not fully satisfied. Political demonstrations, in addition to the high-powered stream of oratory and the rhythmical chanting of slogans, are invariably enlivened by the presence of one, if not two brass bands, while sessions of Parliament, thanks to the high pitch of development to which the slamming of desk-lids and banging of despatch-boxes has here attained, frequently astound even French observers brought up in the hard school of the Chambre des Députés. In everyday life the polite commonplaces of social intercourse are normally exchanged in the ringing tones of Demosthenes sharing his candid opinion of Philip of Macedon with a crowd of several thousands in the open air, and in summer the traveller approaching the coast of Attica across the waters of the Saronic Gulf is frequently puzzled by the continuous buzzing that first becomes audible soon after passing the point of Aegina, increasing in intensity as he draws nearer the shore which, he is startled finally to discover, proceeds from the casual conversation being sustained on the bathing-beaches of Phaleron. Nor is it only the human figures in the landscape who are subject to this weakness, for in Athens, and nowhere else so far as I know, the cocks are accustomed to greet the dawn at all hours of the day and night: as almost all Athenians, even flat-dwellers, are enthusiastic keepers of poultry, this contribution to the general din is not to be despised. Needless to say, while there is every reason for supposing that this passion is deep-seated and of long standing, the modern Greeks with their great powers of rapid assimilation have availed themselves of all the discoveries of modern science to such good purpose that they have far surpassed the best which their great ancestors could achieve. The radio, the gramophone and the internal-combustion engine are all employed to the fullest advantage, but it is noticeable that insofar as modern research has tended towards the elimination of sound its results have been firmly rejected; thus the majority of the Athenian trams are of the oldest and noisiest vintage, and such few comparatively new models as appear on the streets have all, by skilful handling and a few minor adjustments, been rendered in this respect almost as good as old.

Nowhere is this carefully cultivated talent for noise more vigorously, or to the Anglican ear more surprisingly, employed than in the service of religion. Here the very church bells call with an insistent, imperative clang which to those accustomed to the gentle summons from the steeple of St. Fridiswede's sounding softly across the sunset fields of Birckett Forster, would seem more suited to the tocsin than to evensong. (Owing to the rugged nature of Greek political life it must be admitted that they are, in fact, almost as frequently employed for the former task as for the latter.) In many of the monasteries, however, the monks still cling to the older fashion of calling the faithful, traditional in the Orthodox Church, beating on a suspended wooden beam with a hammer, holding that this instrument,

while possibly inferior to the bell in carrying power, is even more insistent at close quarters. In some cases a long iron bar has been substituted for the beam, and the results thus attained are said to be even more satisfactory. But these are merely the everyday routine practices and it is only on the great festivals that one is able to appreciate the real pre-eminence of the Church in this field.

Easter, in the Orthodox Church, far surpasses in importance all other feasts, and in Greece it is celebrated by the whole nation, including even those who for the rest of the year are notoriously indifferent in such matters, with a fervour and intensity considerably greater than that which we are accustomed to display at Christmas. The fast of Lent has been observed in progressive stages, culminating, in Holy Week, for the devout in almost total abstinence and in an absence of meat even on the mondaine dinner-tables of Kolonaki. All Good Friday the bells have tolled ceaselessly from every belfry in Athens, and after dark the Bier has been carried in procession round the confines of every parish. Holy Saturday is a *dies non*; for the only time in the whole year the cafés are empty and even the terrace at Yennaki's is deserted except for a handful of foreigners, while in the church all is dark save for one solitary candle on the altar. Towards midnight the space opposite the great west doors of the Metropolis, and of every church throughout the land, is gradually filled by an immense crowd in whom the fasting of the previous week and the unaccustomed gloom of the day, so foreign to the nature of a people not markedly austere, have induced a nervous condition bordering on hysteria. The wooden platform erected on a line with the high altar is now occupied by members of the government and representatives of the diplomatic corps, the latter holding their candles in the slightly embarrassed manner of grown-ups participating in a game of oranges and lemons, while from the open doors the sound of the chanting which has been going on within the darkened cathedral for many hours takes on a more urgent note. A few minutes before midnight the Archbishop emerges attended by two deacons, one carrying a lighted candle from the altar, and mounting the platform begins the reading of the Gospel. By now a deathly hush, or what passes in Greece for a deathly hush, that is to say an absence of sound that compares not unfavourably with the noise of the small mammal-house on a quiet afternoon, has fallen on the vast crowd, which is maintained unbroken until, on the stroke of midnight, the Bishop pronounces the words "*Xristos anesth*", "Christ is risen". At this the night is rent by a wave of sound in comparison with which all the noises to which one has grown accustomed on other days of the year are as tinkling cymbals. A massed choir and two brass bands burst into powerful, though different, songs of praise; the guard of honour presents arms with a crash unrivalled

even in the Wellington Barracks; every bell in the city, ably assisted by air-raid sirens and factory whistles, clangs out the good news, while the cheering crowds greet their Risen Lord with a barrage of rockets, squibs, Roman candles, Chinese crackers, and volley after volley of small-arms fire discharged by such of the devout, a not inconsiderable proportion, as have come to the ceremony armed.

72

SAILING TO BYZANTIUM

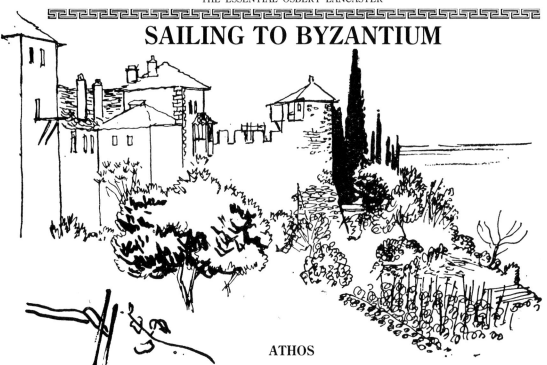

ATHOS

ACCORDING to tradition this strange and extraordinarily beautiful peninsula was first sancti-fied by the Virgin Mary herself, who stopped here on her way from Palestine to Cyprus, and at whose advent all the pagan shrines and statues immediately collapsed. From that time forth, while its sanctity remained inviolate, its history was for several hundred years uneventful, or at least, unrecorded. At the very beginning of the tenth century we hear of various hermits living in the remoter fastnesses of the mountain whose relatively simple and uninstructed life was, towards the end of the century, complicated by the arrival of St. Athanasios. This formidable figure was a monk who had for many years enjoyed a position, *vis-à-vis* that tough but neurotic and unamiable general, Nicephorus Phocas, the liberator of Crete, which would in the West have been described as that of Father Confessor. Encouraged by his Imperial charge, who had long entertained the ambition of devoting himself in old age to the contemplative life, Athanasios descended upon Athos and not only started to organise the rather idiosyncratic practice of monasticism that had hitherto flourished, but started to build a monastery into which his distinguished patron could in due course conveniently retire. But then two events occurred which, fortunately only temporar-ily, disrupted this plan. The middle-aged general fell madly in love with the Empress Theophano who, responding, and her husband conveniently dying, promptly raised Phocas to the purple, an elevation which caused him indefinitely to postpone the fulfilment of his monastic ambitions; and Athanasios, naturally much shaken by this change of plan, returned to Athos where the partially constructed dome of his new foundation fell on him, finally removing his chance of seeing his great work completed, but for ever ensuring his sanctity. However, his enterprise survived him and not only was his own foundation, the Great Lavra, duly completed, but in the following centuries the whole headland was adorned with religious foundations. From then on its history was, by Balkan standards, comparatively

73

tranquil. From time to time pirates descended, occasionally catching a monastery unawares; efforts were made by Iconoclast Emperors to suppress the Holy Pictures, almost always, thanks to the vigilance of the monks and, on many occasions, to the direct intervention of the Panaghia, ineffectual; and the attempts of Latin Emperors to impose the Western rite in due course produced a crop of martyrs, and, it must be admitted, a handful of collaborationists whose indestructible corpses remain in a state of grisly preservation in the Cave of the Wicked Dead. Feuds and disputes between the various monasteries were frequent but only once was the Mountain the scene of a major theological controversy. This arose at the end of the thirteenth century as the result of the emergence of an Athonite sect known as the Hesychasts who maintained that a prolonged and solitary contemplation of the navel would afford to those with sufficient perseverance a glimpse of the Uncreated Light which had irradiated Mount Tabor at the Transfiguration. This belief, at first condemned as heretical, gained many adherents and was finally accepted by the Orthodox Church in the last years of the Empire, but found, not altogether surprisingly, no expression, as far as I am aware, in art.

Today this long ridge, ending in the most dramatic of all mountains, thrusting down into the Aegean, dotted with monasteries, sanctified by innumerable legends, as unrelentingly masculine as White's Club, remains a fascinating but rapidly crumbling fossil, the abiding inspiration of many of the most highly charged writers of our time. While the natural beauty of the place abundantly justifies pages of purple prose, the enthusiasm aroused by its architectural features is harder to understand. Enormously picturesque as most of them are, the majority of the existing monasteries approximate, anyhow at first glance, to superb stage settings; the architectural value of the component parts of these extraordinary ensembles is slight, and they seem to belong rather to the world of Bakst and Bibbienna than to that of Palladio or Philibert de l'Orme.

The customary monastic plan is comparatively simple: a circle, or polygon, of formidable walls, reinforced at intervals by watch-towers, supporting, on the inside, ranges of buildings varying in style from the most primitive adaptations of the traditional Turkish Khan to the most highly sophisticated examples of Tsarist neo-classic, encloses an open space in which stand a canopied fountain, the *phiale*, the *katholikon* or abbey church, a clock-tower, a varying number of chapels and, occasionally, the refectory. Almost all the larger churches are examples of the multi-domed cross-in-square, first developed in the Middle Byzantine period, modified to suit monastic requirements by the addition of semi-circular apses to the north and south arms of the cross. Frequently they possess not only a narthex and exo-narthex, but also a further external porch known as a *lite*. The drums of the dome are polygonal, usually divided by engaged colonettes flanking doubly recessed windows, topped by leaden roofs with undulating cornices. In several cases, notably those foundations which a closeness to the sea rendered unusually exposed to corsair raids, the area covered was comparatively small and the necessary accommodation could only be achieved by building upwards. The result was a series of skyscraper-like towers topped with three or four courses of projecting balconies, producing a strange, Tibetan effect.

The most immediately striking impression produced by all these buildings is that created by the lavish employment of brilliant colour. Elsewhere in the Byzantine world the brick or stonework of church exteriors was normally left uncovered, but here it is almost always concealed beneath a coat of paint regularly renewed. The most popular colours are sang-de-bœuf, a rusty pink, Prussian blue and ochre; even when, usually in the smaller churches, the stonework is visible, the tile-courses are heightened with crimson and picked out in white.

All the churches and some of the refectories are covered internally with murals but, as with the architecture, it is the general overall effect which impresses rather than single scenes or portraits. On Athos, where the ancient customs and practices of the Orthodox Church are more stubbornly upheld than elsewhere, the traditional attitude to paintings has always prevailed: cleaning is taboo, and when age, damp and candle-smoke have reduced the legibility of a picture to the point where the subject matter is visible only to the eye of faith, it has firmly been repainted. Thus, while the lines and composition of the original have usually been faithfully ahered to, colour and tone values have undergone surprising changes, and in many cases what we see today stands in the same relationship to the original as an eighteenth-century English copy of a sixteenth-century Italian Madonna made from a line engraving. If and when some of the finest of the early series, notably those at Vatopedi, have received the expert treatment to which, at the time of my last visit, the icons at the Great Lavra were being subjected, the enthusiasm they aroused in the late Robert Byron and other experts may well be shared by the layman.

Compared, say, with that of Cluny in the West, the architectural and artistic influence of Athos in the Byzantine world was nil. It originated no new forms or plans and during long centuries hardly modified those it had originally inherited from elsewhere; even the layout of the monastic buildings, which was faithfully copied in Bulgaria and elsewhere in

75

the Balkans, had been evolved in Syria and developed in southern Greece centuries before the coming of Athanasios to Chalkidiki. After the fall of the Empire, life continued almost exactly as before; the community's relations with the Turks were always surprisingly good and the suzerainty of the Sultan, who never attempted to interfere in matters of doctrine or internal discipline, may well have come to seem less irksome than that of the Thirteenth Apostle. Isolation from the contemporary world was now complete and in this strange Byzantine enclave in an Islamic Empire there flourished, at a slowly diminishing tempo, a way of life that, save in a few remote spots such as Sinai, had elsewhere become extinct. From time to time there came travellers and bibliophiles from the West who relieved the monks of manuscripts and other treasures the significance of which they had in most cases long since ceased to understand; frescoes were duly renewed and buildings restored and added to in the traditional manner, and, indeed, most of what we see today dates from the twilight years. To describe in detail all the twenty remaining monasteries would, in a work such as this, be tedious and unjustified; I have accordingly selected four which seem to me to be those likely to prove most rewarding for the ordinary visitor, who should, however, be warned that even this reduced round will need time, for not only are mules no longer readily available but at all seasons sudden changes of wind are liable to render the small harbours and anchorages inaccessible. Not only are stout legs and a strong stomach essential but also high spirits, for a powerful melancholy haunts these slopes, and nowhere in the whole Mediterranean does the heart sink so regularly with the sun.

The Protaton. The administrative capital of Athos is the mournful, if picturesque, little village of Caryes. Here are the residence of the civil governor and the assembly-hall of the representatives of the leading monasteries. Opposite the latter stands the church of the Protaton, probably the oldest existing building on the Mountain, so called from the Protos or first among the brethren to whom the supreme authority was formerly delegated. Alone among the churches of Athos it is a basilica, and its foundation predates the coming of Athanasios who enlarged it, round about A.D. 965, with funds provided by Nicephorus Phocas. At the end of the thirteenth century it was badly damaged by fire or earthquake but soon restored and decorated with the existing frescoes.

The artist responsible was, according to a long and well-attested tradition, Pansellinos of Thessaloniki, one of the comparatively few Byzantine artists whose identity has survived. However, as the laudatory references to him date largely from the eighteenth century and, while establishing his personality, fail to mention the exact period at which he flourished, his connection with these particular paintings had formerly to be taken on trust. Recently, however, a careful comparison with contemporary work in Thessaloniki (notably in the Euthymios chapel in S. Demetrios) which all traditions agree was his place of origin, has strengthened the probability of his responsibility. The paintings themselves are among the earliest and finest examples of the Macedonian school, which flourished during the Palaeologan period, chiefly in northern Greece, Macedonia and Serbia, but of which the influence extended as far south as Mistra. It was characterised by a light palette, a tendency

to generalisation, a fondness for large, open forms, and an intensity, particularly in portraiture, almost amounting to expressionism. (The Macedonian artist's approach to his subject matter is sometimes, rather misleadingly, described as realistic, a qualification which can only be justified by comparison with that of the opposing Cretan school.) Here the unusual layout of the frescoes arises from the difficulty of modifying a system evolved for the decoration of the domed cross-in-square to suit a basically basilican plan; they are in four zones, the topmost filled with the ancestors of Christ from Adam onwards, the second with scenes from the life of Christ, the third, which is broken on three sides by arches, by the four Evangelists, and on the unbroken west wall by the Dormition of the Virgin; the lowest and widest is taken up with a whole portrait gallery of saints, hermits and Fathers of the Church. The most interesting and original of these four series is the second, where the various traditional episodes do not occupy self-contained panels, as was the usual practice, but are linked by smaller subsidiary scenes into one continuous narrative band.

While for anyone seriously interested in the development of Byzantine painting a visit to the Protaton is essential, the enthusiast should be warned that the whereabouts of the key is, even by Athonite standards, exceptionally difficult to establish. Indeed, I myself was quite unable to locate it, and the above account is based on what can be seen by energetic clambering up to windows, and on the evidence of the collection of admirable copies made by Mr. Photis Zachariou, reproduced in my friend Professor Xyngopoulos' informative account of Pansellinos.

The Great Lavra. The monastery of the Great Lavra is the oldest, richest and most important on Athos. It is not, however, the most beautiful. Large as is the area covered by its courtyard, it is not large enough comfortably to accommodate the quantity of buildings with which it is adorned and, while picturesque corners abound, the total effect is jumbled and confused. The *katholikon*, dedicated to the Dormition of the Virgin, is the model for almost all the churches on the Mountain, a domed cross-in-square with round apses on the cross-arms, a polygonal apse on the east and a domed narthex and exo-narthex on the west. Whether or not due to the efforts of those responsible for the rebuilding to prevent any repetition of the disaster which overwhelmed the founder, the dome seems almost too solid and the overall proportions clumsy. It is painted blood-red without, and within is covered with murals by the celebrated Cretan painter Theophanes dating from the tenth

century. Whether, as some maintain, these have remained untouched since they were painted, or, as Robert Byron claimed, were heavily restored in the eighteenth century, they have certainly not been cleaned for a very long time. As the Cretan school habitually employed a far more sombre range of colours than the Macedonian, relying on a technique of carefully spaced highlights on a very dark under-painting, the total effect is one of gorgeous gloom in which details are hard to distinguish. The finest single scene, as I remember, is that of the Transfiguration. The exo-narthex was rebuilt early in the nineteenth century and later enlivened with the existing frescoes, usually dismissed as beneath contempt, but which include some little landscape panels in an almost Braque-like range of blacks, umbers and venetian red, which may be only folk-art but possess undoubted charm. Adjoining the main church are two chapels, one dedicated to the Forty Martyrs, the other to St. Nicholas; the former marks the spot where St. Athanasios suffered his fatal accident, the latter is decorated, rather prettily, with murals by another Cretan painter, Frangopoulos.

Of the rest of the various buildings enclosed in the great courtyard the most remarkable is the refectory opposite the *katholikon*. A cruciform building with an apse to accommodate the abbot's seat at the head of the cross, a splendid wooden roof and completely frescoed walls, it was built, or rather rebuilt, in the sixteenth century by Archbishop Gennadios of Serres. The best of the paintings are the entombment of Athanasios, a splendidly composed scene on a big scale, and a terrifying Doom of which the layout recalls that at Torcello, although it is far less accomplished, is in painting, not mosaic, and is nearly three centuries later in date. But finally, it is not any individual scene which remains in the mind so much as the completeness and consistency of the whole achievement, suggesting, as it does, a setting from some sumptuous production of *Boris Godunov*. Owing to the fact that the Lavra has long since abandoned the coenobitic rule for the idiorhythmic, whereby the monks are allowed to take their meals in their own cells, it now seldom fulfils its original function.

Between the refectory and the church stands the *phiale*, perhaps the most beautiful of any on Athos. The basin is enclosed by a series of marble slabs, carved with the usual Byzantine motifs, and covered by a Turkish-style dome resting on a ring of pillars with elaborate capitals; it is flanked by two immensely old cypresses, said to have been planted by St. Athanasios and his companion St. Euthymios, one of which, when last I saw it, was going rapidly home.

Dionysiou. Not only is this the most beautifully situated of all the Athonite monasteries— perched on a high, impregnable rock overlooking the sea, its balconies and domes airborne on massive stone towers—but the one which most powerfully radiates an atmosphere of serenity and devotion. The abbot, when I was there, was a personage of great dignity and exceptional intelligence; not only was he fully aware of the value, both religious and aesthetic, of his house's treasures, but was possessed of a truly oecumenical spirit nourished by close contacts with All Saints', Margaret Street. The librarian was young, enthusiastic and had extremely clean hands, the food was plain but good and all the monks we met took a modest, unboastful pride in their monastery, such as one rarely encounters in the idiorhythmic houses.

Owing to the narrowness of the site there is here no vast courtyard with free-standing buildings, but a highly picturesque ecclesiastical warren on several levels. Founded towards the end of the fourteenth century by one of the Greek Emperors of Trebizond, the monastery fortunately escaped those devastating fires which regularly ravaged so many of

its rivals and, until very recently when, to judge from photographs, a rather unfortunate concrete extension was added to one corner, had suffered comparatively little reconstruction. The church follows the usual plan, with additional domes over the *prothesis* and *diakonikon*, and is painted the familiar sang-de-bœuf in striking contrast to the adjacent arcaded passages (sometimes improperly referred to as cloisters) which are a very brilliant burnt orange. Inside there are paintings by another Cretan named Zorzi, rather lighter in tone and a great deal cleaner than those in the Lavra. There is also a T-shaped refectory frescoed with saints and martyrdoms which, as Dionysiou has never abandoned the coenobitic rule, is in regular use. On the back wall of the passage leading to it is an elaborate Doom wherein one of the devils is emitting an unquestionably mushroom-shaped cloud. The abbot, who carefully drew our attention to it, regarded this as a clear warning of the coming nuclear holocaust in which most of the civilised world would be destroyed, but from which the Holy Mountain had been assured of Divine Protection. This cheerful conclusion provoked a pitying smile and a withering German comment on the abbot's credulity from the insufferable Lutheran student who had attached himself to us; personally I had an uneasy feeling that the good man might well be on to something.

Of the carefully preserved treasures the most beautiful is a superb Imperial chrysobul establishing and guaranteeing the monastery's foundation, one of the great masterpieces of Byzantine illumination; the most fascinating, a tusk of that strangest of all Orthodox saints, S. Cristophoros Cynocephalos, the dog-headed St. Christopher, a young man of exceptional physical beauty who, fearing lest he should prove a standing temptation to both sexes, prayed for, and was granted, this alarming transformation.

Vatopedi. Seen from afar Vatopedi has the appearance of some enormous fortified manor house, or possibly a small town, with little to suggest its religious character. From the tiny harbour a path winds upwards to a large gateway, rather incongruously decorated with some unfortunate coloured glass, from which a strategically planned tunnel leads into one  of the most extraordinary open spaces in the world.

"The irregular enclosure in which we now found ourselves covered an area of perhaps a couple of acres. The ground rose sharply on one side giving to that section of the encompassing wall and its adjoining buildings a cliff-like height, the effect of which had been artificially emphasised by setting the cobblestones in a great radiating arc, diminishing in numbers with the gradient, which recalled, although there the device is employed, as it were, in the reverse direction, the Piazza della Signoria in Siena. That, at first glance, was all that I was able distinctly to take in. The rest was a great, jumbled impression, quite staggering in its impact, of domes and arches, of ill-supported balconies projecting at improbable angles and perilous heights, of stone ramps and outside staircases, of free-standing churches in shocking-pink and wide-eaved, spiky-roofed clock-towers and, right at the far end, closing the vista, of a huge, arcaded, many-domed building freshly painted a vivid sang-de-bœuf. The only structure which even remotely suggested the non-Byzantine world, although without striking any jarring note of direct incongruity, was a large, many-storeyed, greystone block, immediately to our right, in a tolerably correct version of neo-classic with pilasters and pediments but saved from any hint of academicism by the bold use of white plastered pointing and the liberal application of light Prussian blue to mouldings and surrounds." [*Cornhill Magazine*, Spring 1958]

Vatopedi, although second to the Great Lavra in monastic precedence, is the largest of all the monasteries, among which it occupies a socially predominant position analogous to that of Christ Church among the colleges of Oxford. Discounting improbable stories that connect it with the fifth-century Empress Pulcheria, its foundation came immediately after that of the Lavra at the end of the tenth century. The church, which is dedicated to the Annunciation, is a larger, more skilful version of that at the Lavra, and architecturally the finest on the Mountain. Painted sang-de-bœuf, the exterior is animated by the eye of God in a triangle in the centre of the façade, gazing down with, in these surroundings, a strangely Protestant, almost Masonic, fixity.

The interior, which is splendidly proportioned on the grandest scale, is completely covered with paintings of the Macedonian school, contemporary with those in the Protaton, but the majority repainted in the eighteenth century. Personally I find the enthusiasm they aroused in the late Robert Byron, who held that they were the supreme masterpiece of that school, hard to share; grandly conceived and competently carried out, in their present condition they seem to me to be constricted by a certain academicism. However, this may well be due to the eighteenth-century restorers, for it is notable that the paintings in the exo-narthex, which, so it is maintained, have never been repainted, are far lighter in tone and more consciously monumental in treatment than the rest, approximating more closely to contemporary work in the Protaton.

Grand and splendid as is the existing decoration, it may well have fallen short of the original intention of the founders. Over the entrance from the narthex into the main body of the church are some splendid mosaics in lunettes. Whether they are all that remain of the original scheme, or whether for some reason that scheme was abandoned in favour of fresco before it had been carried further, is not clear; various dates, ranging from the eleventh to the fourteenth century, have been suggested but the earlier would appear to be the more likely.

The collection of relics and treasures housed at Vatopedi has long been the envy of all the other houses on Athos, including as it does the Virgin's girdle and a large fragment of the True Cross. From a purely aesthetic point of view the most rewarding are some icons, donated by the Iconodule Empress Theodora (possibly those which, as related in the well-known anecdote, the court-dwarf reported to her inconoclast husband she was hiding); some very beautiful, if alarmingly painstaking, portable mosaics; and a porphyry cup donated

by the Despot of Epirus which has been accorded extravagant admiration by Western pilgrims. But for me the high-water mark among all these minor masterpieces is achieved by a series of small gold panels, embossed with the figures of saints, which have been incorporated into the frame of a reliquary; dating, I imagine, from the nineth or tenth century they are exquisite without being precious, monumental although miniature, supreme examples of a craft of which the Byzantines were always masters.

Other buildings in the great courtyard include sixteen churches (so it is claimed, but I have never counted), a fine fifteenth-century clock-tower, the oldest on the Mountain, and an elaborate *phiale*, the canopy of which is supported on a ring of coupled columns. The refectory was completely and very dully frescoed in the eighteenth century which also saw the erection of the ruined theological college outside the walls.

MISTRA

This extraordinary dead city, set on a steep, sunbaked mountainside with its vertiginous, crumbling walls, its ruined cisterns and foundations treacherously masked by thyme and Jerusalem sage, and its quantity of churches, is today principally celebrated for its wall-paintings. These are numerous, frequently fine, and have given rise to more controversy than perhaps any other group of frescoes in the world. The dates, the artists and, above all, the merits of these works have been, and continue to be, matters for the liveliest dispute; Byron and Talbot-Rice, Diehl and Millet, Muratoff and Grabar, all support different theories and roundly condemn each other's conclusions. At Mistra the conscientious art-lover is not just advised but compelled to use his own judgement.

SS. Theodoroi. This, the earliest of the Mistra churches, despite the fact that it was built around 1290, that is to say under the Palaeologues, conforms closely both in layout and decoration to the churches of the preceding period. The octagonal plan is similar to that of Daphni and the exterior is enriched with herringbone brickwork, dog-tooth bands and high-shouldered windows, as at Merbaka, and the lancets in the drum, which is dodecagonal, are separated by blank niches as at Hagia Moni. The church, which has recently been repaired, was roofless for many years and the remaining paintings, which include a portrait of Manuel Palaeologos kneeling before Our Lord, have suffered in consequence. In the pavement a double-headed eagle commemorates the coronation of the last Byzantine Emperor.

The Metropolis or S. Demetrios. The present church, which was built early in the fourteenth century by Archbishop Nicephoros Moschopoulos, replaced an earlier basilical structure, some fragments of which it incorporates. The better and earlier of the two groups of paintings are those in the *bema*; dignified and hieratic, they are, despite their comparatively late date, quite uninfluenced by the humanistic tendencies of the Palaeologan revival and might well have been painted a hundred or more years earlier. Particularly impressive is the Virgin in the apse, statuesque and remote, recalling Torcello. In the dome is a fine Hetoimasia with angels, perhaps the latest example of a theme very popular in the early period of Byzantine art. The remaining paintings in the *naos* and narthex, scenes from the Life of Christ and the Martyrdom of St. Demetrios, are later in date and probably the work of an artist of the Macedonian school.

The whole cycle of paintings in this church is generally dismissed as stiff and uninteresting, notably by Byron and Talbot-Rice, but is considered by Muratoff to be the finest in Mistra.

The Brontocheion or Aphendiko. The Brontocheion was the richest and most important monastery in the Morea and this church, built a year or two later than the Metropolis, was suitably impressive and perhaps the last ever to be enriched with marble revetment (now vanished). The plan is of the greatest interest; basilical at ground-level and cruciform above, it recalls that of S. Irene at Constantinople, with the addition of domes over the angle-chambers, and may be regarded as a classic example of that tendency towards revivalism that recurred from time to time throughout Byzantine history. To my mind the interior is architecturally the finest of any church in Mistra; the arcades cutting off the transepts from the *naos* are beautifully proportioned and exactly related to the galleries

above, and one here has the feeling, only induced by first-rate buildings, that the problem of space has been fully understood and brilliantly solved.

The paintings are fragmentary and not too well preserved and, while individually they do not compare with the finest of the single scenes in the Peribleptos and the Pantanassa, I have the impression that, when complete, the whole cycle was probably rather satisfactory in relationship to the architecture. The most impressive of those that remain are the head of the priest Zacharias in one of the domes and a remarkable composition in a small side chamber in which *chrysobuls*, or imperial edicts, are unrolled by angels. Today the church is no longer in the appalling condition which justifiably excited the righteous indignation of Robert Byron; admirably restored, the hideous new tiles are the only feature likely to arouse criticism.

The Evangelistra. This church, not far from the Metropolis, is probably a funerary chapel dating from the early fourteenth century. Cross-in-square in plan, it is built of dressed stones pointed with tiles, has three projecting apses and an octagonal drum on which the line of the eaves is broken by the projecting archivolts of the four windows that alternate with niches. Externally it produces a rather muddled effect owing both to the site and to additional buildings, and the interior is of no great interest.

Hagia Sophia. Built in 1350 by Manuel Cantacuzenos, immediately above the Palace of the Despots, this was the court church. Its plan resembles that of the Evangelistra and the exterior is similarly cluttered up with ossuaries and *parekklesions*. Formerly it was in a semi-ruinous condition and only traces of wall-paintings appear to have survived, but it has recently been restored and more paintings, reportedly of some merit, have been discovered under coats of whitewash in a side-chapel.

The Peribleptos. Basically, the church, which probably dates from the middle of the fourteenth century, is a cross-in-square with a prolonged western arm and no narthex, but the plan is complicated by an additional chamber to the north, an irregular *parekklesion* on the west, and the fact that it is partially cut out of the hillside. On the main apse is a fleur-de-lis between rosettes which, together with a trefoil on an adjacent tower and the prolongation of the nave, suggest Western influence.

On the first entering, the interior seems dark, mysterious and predominantly blue, and it is some moments before one becomes fully aware of the wealth of painting that surrounds one. According to Millet there were two artists engaged, one conforming to the Cretan tradition, whose work displays extraordinary delicacy and finish, the other employing a looser, more impressionistic technique and possibly influenced by the Macedonian school. The former's masterpiece is the Divine Liturgy in the main apse where Our Lord, robed as a priest, celebrates beneath a *ciborium*, flanked by a procession of angels with blue and green wings clad in long white surplices; the painting of these last, and the suggestion of the form and movement underneath them, is a technical feat of the highest order, and the whole scene must rank amongst the finest achievements of Byzantine painting. Hardly less impressive are the Transfiguration in the adjacent aisle, with its intense figure of Christ surrounded by a great mandorla and the scene of the two Marys at the Empty Tomb, in which the pose and placing of the angel are almost exactly paralleled in a picture of the same subject by Duccio in Siena, painted nearly a century earlier. (Any direct influence need not, however, be assumed; probably both artists were working from illuminated manuscripts deriving from the same original source.)

Of the other group the most striking, to my mind, is the Entry into Jerusalem, dominated by the figure in the foreground wearing a boldly striped cloak.

The Monastery of the Pantanassa. The earlier fifteenth-century church of this little monastery, which still shelters a handful of nuns, is architecturally the most interesting, if not the most beautiful, of all the Mistra churches. Terraced on a steeply sloping hillside, it is not properly orientated; the axis is closer to north–south than to east–west, and it is equipped with a loggia, similar perhaps to that which once existed alongside the Brontocheion and with a campanile of a decidedly Western character. Externally the three apses are decorated with two bands of blind arcading, the upper of the normal round-headed Byzantine type, the lower of narrow lancets topped by pointed arches, which are separated by a border of strap-work loops, slightly out of proportion to the rest of the ornamentation, terminating in flower-like finials. The overall effect is rather that of some neo-Gothic folly or toll-house conceived by Batty Langley.

The plan is of the same revivalist type as that of the Brontocheion with galleries and narthex (the exo-narthex has vanished). Of the domes only the largest, and that over the central bay of the narthex, project externally, the remainder being covered by a continuous roof, a sure sign of Western influence.

The numerous paintings still adorning the interior are regarded by some as the finest flowering of the Palaeologan revival, foreshadowing the Italian Renaissance; others prefer the quieter colouring and less demonstrative quality of those in the Peribleptos. What, however, in both series is most likely to strike the visitor who is not a *kunstforscher*, is not so much signs of a new humanistic approach, as the fidelity with which the old, prescribed, formulae are still adhered to. In the Nativity, the Virgin lies diagonally in the usual rocky cleft, with the two attendants preparing to wash the Babe in the foreground, the Magi popping up from behind the cardboard mountains on the left, and the angels, shepherds and cattle all in their accustomed places as they are at Hosios Loukas, Daphni and in innumerable manuscripts; in the Entry into Jerusalem the same figure in the same striped cloak dominates the foreground and the Presentation in the Temple takes place against those same strangely curved architectural elements which occur both in S. Mark's and the Kahriye Djami. Such extreme conformity might well have produced an inhibiting effect (as it undoubtedly did in Ancient Egypt), but the Byzantine experience successfully demonstrates that for the first-rate artist who is not a genius it may well prove a source of strength; freed from any obsessive urge to be original at all costs, he can concentrate on intensifying the internal significance of the scene by his handling of paint and colour, and by inconspicuous personal re-adjustments within the accepted and clearly defined compositional framework provided and enforced by ecclesiastical tradition.

MONEMVASIA

Far down on the easternmost prong of the Peloponnese there rises, just off-shore, but joined to the mainland by a causeway, the great rock of Monemvasia. Heavily fortified from an early period, it was captured from the Greeks by William de Villehardouin in 1249 after a prolonged siege, but less than twenty years later was returned by treaty at the same time as Mistra. In 1464 it fell to the Venetians, in 1540 to the Turks, back to the Venetians in 1690, and finally to the Turks in 1715. With this history, it is hardly surprising that the architectural tradition is not distinguished by continuity.

In the lower town are four churches of which the identification is not rendered any easier by the fact that no two guide-books, and few of the inhabitants, agree on the dedications. Of these, three are of the same type, all late in date, one having been built during the final Venetian occupation, and showing strong traces of Western influence. The circumference of the drum is rather larger than that of the dome, which itself rests on pointed arches and is left unroofed and faced with cement, as are the barrel vaults over the arms of the cross (churches of an exactly similar kind occur frequently in Cyprus at the same date). The largest of these may safely be identified as the Metropolis, thanks to the presence over the west door of a Byzantine slab decorated with peacocks which was mentioned by Colonel Leake. Inside, the iconostasis is adorned with some very late icons, heavily, and to me unfortunately, influenced by the Venetian Renaissance. The fourth church in the lower town, although probably of even later date, has a more familiar aspect. It is cross-in-square in plan and decorated externally in stripes of yellow, white and blue; within is to be found a miraculous icon, the handiwork, so it is said, of St. Luke himself, which was drawn up from the sea in a bucket and still commands the veneration of the few remaining inhabitants of this picturesque but melancholy stronghold.

On the very summit of the rock, surrounded by ruinous curtain-walls and fortified gates, rises the great Church of Hagia Sophia, most spectacularly situated of all Byzantine places of worship, built by Andronicus the Second in the late thirteenth century. For its date both the plan and decoration are old-fashioned, akin to Daphni and Hosios Loukas; the drum is polygonal, the dome rests on an octagon and the transepts have three-light windows. The most unusual feature is the row of short, flat-topped openings enriched with Renaissance mouldings, now blocked up, which once connected the galleries with a much later narthex, an insertion dating from Venetian times. There are also some good carved stonework and the remains of wall-paintings, also rather old-fashioned, mostly of martyrs. Exhausted as the visitor may be by the climb, he should on no account fail to go round to the north side of the church, where a small terrace crowns a great cliff with a sheer drop of 800 ft. to the ultramarine below.

A drawing of which Osbert was particularly proud, done as a present for Anne Scott-James.

EGYPT

Osbert's drawings of Egypt and the Middle East anticipate those which David Hockney was later to make in preparation for his illustrations to the poems of Cavafy and on commission for the *Sunday Times*. What the two artists have in common is the ability to catch both the impressive and the comic aspects of the region.

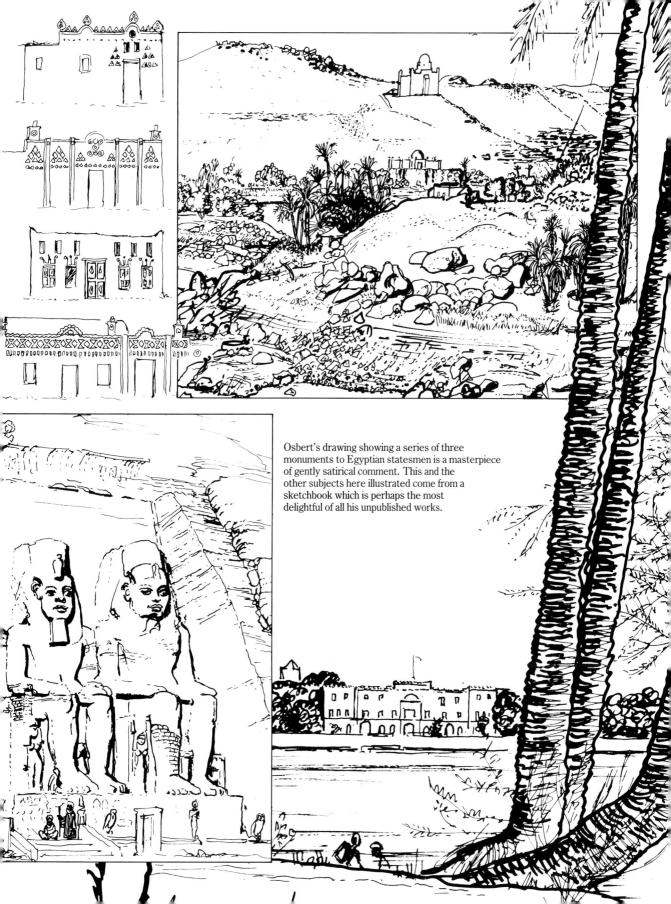

Osbert's drawing showing a series of three
monuments to Egyptian statesmen is a masterpiece
of gently satirical comment. This and the
other subjects here illustrated come from a
sketchbook which is perhaps the most
delightful of all his unpublished works.

91

LEVANTINE
AFTERNOON

THE lofty column, moss bedeckt,
   Where once a sainted stylite sat
   Displays a summons to elect
An unattractive Democrat.

Above the shrine of Artemis
The English church, by G. E. Street,
Proclaims, with Gothic emphasis,
A faith which triumphs over heat.

Here past and present, side by side,
In perfect amity are met;
The call to prayer is amplified
In every Mosque and minaret.

And placid Turks distribute Marshall Aid
Playing backgammon in a plane-tree's shade.

DRUNK
ON YE
SABBATH

THE ENGLISH OBSERVED

Osbert Lancaster's consciousness of his own identity as an Englishman did not prevent him turning a sardonic eye on the foibles of his fellow countrymen—not to mention his fellow countrywomen. He became expert at dissecting their manners and mores, seeming to do so with particularly relish when he was addressing an American audience. The audience at home he addressed chiefly through the medium of the pocket cartoons which he did over so many years for the *Daily Express*. The latter fall into several categories: some are direct comments on matters of the day; others build up an elaborate fantasy about English upper and upper middle-class life. Fond childhood memories of the two species in question seem to be responsible for the frequent appearances made in these cartoons by formidable dowagers and by members of the Anglican clergy. The cartoons in which they feature carry distinct echoes of Oscar Wilde's marvellous comedy, *The Importance of Being Earnest*.

KEYS TO UNDERSTANDING THE ENGLISH

Article written for *The New York Times,* 1948

ONE of the most widespread illusions about the English is that they are a very numerous race; an illusion in which the foreign visitor, noticing the thronged streets of the capital and the almost continuous lines of houses alongside the railway, is frequently confirmed for life and which even many of the natives unthinkingly accept. It is only when one tries to isolate an Englishman or seeks to hear a proud statement of his nationality from his own lips, that it becomes apparent how rare a bird one is pursuing. "Well, of course," says one, "my family are really Irish by origin." "My mother's family, you know," remarks another, "all came from Scotland," while a third confesses, with a smile of infinite roguishness, "I suppose I shouldn't really say it, but we have a touch of gypsy blood on my father's side."

This desperate anxiety to disclaim at all costs any suggestion of Anglo-Saxon racial purity springs, I fancy, from the deep-seated romanticism of the English. They are no more backward, although perhaps somewhat subtler in their methods, than any other nation in claiming moral virtues peculiar to themselves, but the ideal which they seek to project, and in which, indeed, they firmly believe, is estimable rather than exciting. Kindly, tolerant, dogged and plain-spoken, John Bull, although a myth-figure, is hardly a romantic conception, and thus, while the average Englishman feels it would be most improper not to identify himself with the national hero, he seeks to satisfy his craving for romance by glamorizing his personal interpretation of the role with the aid of a small dose of what is generally accepted as "romantic" blood.

The comparative degrees of romance attaching to the various races with which the English have most frequently intermarried afford an interesting and instructive study. First come the Irish, for, while as a nation they are quite singularly unsympathetic to the English—and to be wholly Irish is considered by no means a social advantage—the possession of an Irish great-grandmother is held to be an inestimable boon providing just the right leaven of recklessness and charm. Next come the Scots, but in this instance it must be born in mind that for the Englishman all Scots are Highlanders, and a Scots grandfather, even if, as is highly probable, he were in life a Lowland businessman from Sauchiehall Street (and, therefore, just about as romantic as a plate of cold porridge), invariably flourishes in the lively imagination of his descendants fully equipped with kilt and sporran.

The Welsh, curiously enough, although undeniably romantic (singing all those hymns and dressing up as Druids), are rather less popular as forebears, and Welsh blood is almost invariably referred to by its possessors as "a Celtic strain". Gypsy,

The average Briton insists on at least one "romantic" forebear in the family tree.

95

The Englishman's profound horror of any sartorial ostentation . . . Fostered by education,

reinforced by tradition,

at every stage of his career,

FIAT JUSTITIA ETC.

IN MEMORIAM
THE
RIGHT HONOURABLE
THE VISCOUNT
STILT

and common to all classes

of society

in every part

of the United Kingdom

naturally makes it very difficult for him to comprehend the foreigner's passion for fancy dress.

The British regard communion with dumb animals as the best type of social amenity.

American, French (if Huguenot) and Spanish ancestors, although rarer, are all counted romantic and are therefore popular, but Norman blood, due to a steady overvaluation throughout the Victorian Era, has slumped badly and few are now sufficiently unselfconscious to claim it. Australian ancestors are decidedly tricky, while it is perfectly all right, indeed socially advantageous, to possess a great-grandfather who was sent out to Australia, one that came back from that land of opportunity is seldom regarded as a cause for satisfaction.

Having noticed the peculiar pride with which the English lay claim to foreign origins, the stranger might well be misled into supposing that the attitude of the natives towards foreigners will be distinguished by a rather higher degree of appreciation and understanding than elsewhere. It will not, alas, take very long for him to disprove this happy assumption, for while a single foreigner tucked away in a genealogical tree is one thing, a flesh-and-blood example standing on the doorstep is regarded as quite another.

The English are not, as is frequently assumed, actuated by any dislike of foreigners, but they are invariably acutely embarrassed by them. Any persons suffering from the appalling disability of not being English are immediately compared to animals, with which, as is well known, the English have a peculiar sympathy, and the comparison invariably works to the disadvantage of the foreigner. For animals can almost always be relied upon to remain comparatively mute (the adjective "dumb" in the phrase "dumb animals" is one of the highest approbation), but with a foreigner one can never be absolutely certain of enjoying that completely silent communion of great minds, which is, theoretically, the Englishman's conception of the highest form of social intercourse, for some of the species have been known to acquire a considerable knowledge of English.

This is peculiarly undesirable for two reasons: on the one hand, while the Englishman is seldom as averse to conversation as he likes to pretend, he is an exceedingly lazy conversationalist and dislikes having to expand the clipped shorthand in which he normally converses for the benefit of a foreigner who, as he fully realises, can hardly be expected to follow arguments so expressed; on the other hand, if the foreigner turns out to be completely fluent, the Englishman is bitterly resentful at being deprived of the never-failing source of simple fun afforded by a comic accent and is obscurely frightened lest he be the victim of some confidence trick.

Of all the foreigners who visit England, the American finds himself in the most difficult position. Reasonably assuming that the possession of a common tongue will render his path easier, he suffers the more grievous disappointment. The trouble here arises from the fact that, while some few Englishmen are more at ease with foreigners than the majority, almost all, high and low, suffer from a complete disability to distinguish one sort of foreigner from another and accord the term itself the widest possible definition. Not only are Americans, Irish, French, Chinese and Welsh all equally foreign and unaccountable, but, in some parts of the country, Londoners, Yorkshiremen or even the inhabitants of a village a dozen miles away are included in the term. Furthermore, the American, alone among

The passionate insistence on fresh air in midwinter is a cherished peculiarity of the race.

foreigners, suffers, thanks to Hollywood, the disadvantage, once his nationality has been clearly established, of being expected to conform to a generally accepted pattern of behavior. If he does not chew gum, look like one of the better-known film stars and employ the conversation style of the late Damon Runyon, the natives feel cheated and resentful.

Even when the intelligent visitor has accepted the peculiarities of the national attitude toward foreigners, he may still be puzzled and hurt by the seeming unfriendliness that normally prevails in trains and on other similar occasions which have always seemed to him to provide welcome opportunities for enjoyable discourse. This guarded silence, universally maintained in public, may well appear churlish to those who do not realize that the earliest instruction which every English child receives is a solemn warning against "being spoken to by strangers". As a result there is not an occupant of any railway carriage in England who does not at once assume, at least subconsciously, that a casual remark on the weather or a request for the time is the certain prelude to physical assault or at the very least the three-card trick.

Railway travel, indeed, may well prove among the most enlightening, if trying, experiences for the visiting foreigner. Here can be studied, as nowhere else to such advantage, some of the most cherished peculiarities of the island race. The passion for fresh air in midwinter, for instance, which, at the first hint of autumn, causes all the windows in trains and buses and taxis, that have been jammed tight shut all summer long, to be forced down and wedged open, so to remain until the coming of spring, is here very strikingly exemplified.

Another, perhaps more engaging, aspect of the English temperament that is commonly displayed in trains is that governing the English attitude toward children. In life as opposed to literature, the English do not romanticize the young, whom they regard as being simply smaller and nastier editions of their parents. Thus the infants in railway carriages, while being no less numerous or sticky than those in other countries, enjoy far less license to make life intolerable, and the Englishman, when faced with the alternative of allowing little Willy's whining monologue to continue uninterrupted from Crewe to King's Cross or causing some permanent injury to the little lad's libido by an unkind word or a clip on the ear, does not hesitate for a moment.

The inability to distinguish between various species of foreigners, although exceedingly widespread among even the most travelled English, is not quite universal. In every generation there occurs a handful of people whose marked predilection for one single foreign race is almost sufficient to outweigh the prevailing indifference of the majority of the population and is quite likely, in the long run, to prove even more disastrous in its results.

In order to qualify for the sympathy of these professional xenophiles a nation must be small, oppressed and romantic: the choice is thus strictly limited. All the more populous countries are ruled out on the score of size; the Swiss, the Dutch and the Belgians, although limited in numbers, are considered to be insufficiently, or only spasmodically, oppressed. The Czechs, the Jews and the Armenians, although amply fulfilling the first two requirements, have never been regarded as romantic. (If only the Czechs had conformed more closely to the English conception of a romantic race, the whole history of modern Europe might well have been totally different.) The most favored nations are therefore reduced, generally speaking, to the Arabs, the Greeks and the Poles in the permanently established class, with the Hungarians, the Irish and the Spanish occupying a position analogous to that of country members who are allowed all the club privileges for short periods at long intervals.

The English eccentrics who cultivate these enthusiasms, although strictly limited in numbers, are easily distinguishable from the vast majority of their fellow-countrymen. The males, when not undertaking arduous journeys in the countries of their choice, are forever writing to *The Times* newspaper long letters denouncing the policy of His Majesty's Government toward their protégés and presiding over protest meetings and relief committees in all the principal public halls of the land. The females, while sharing to a certain extent in these last activities, proclaim their affections by plastering their homes with peasant pottery and sad little watercolors of Epirus or Damascus or Krakow and by assuming, on the slightest provocation and with no thought of personal appearance, the more involved and highly colored costumes of their adopted countries.

British females love to take up (in costume) the cause of the small and oppressed nation.

Fortunately the number of English xenophiles is, as has been already made clear, very small, and the foreigner who does not belong to one of the chosen nations stands a good chance of being spared their dangerous enthusiasms. Provided such a one does not expect too much, bears in mind that the pursuit of happiness, however worthy an occupation it may have seemed to many estimable men, strikes the English as certainly trivial and probably immoral, and realizes that comfort is something which, according to the English, belongs essentially to the home and must not be looked for outside it, he will not find life among the natives wholly unrewarding. He will not, certainly, be accorded the consideration which is regularly paid to dogs, but his lot will prove far less arduous than that of the children.

ENGLISH AFTERNOON

In 1910 a royal princess
Contracted measles here;
Last spring a pregnant stewardess
Was found beneath the pier;
Her throat, according to the Press,
Was slit from ear to ear.

In all the years that passed between
These two distressing dates
Our only tragedy has been
The rising of the rates,
Though once a flying-bomb was seen
Far out across the straits.

Heard on this coast, the music of the spheres
Would sound like something from *The Gondoliers*.

The drawings on these two pages are
illustrations to *The Pleasure Garden*, done
in collaboration with Anne Scott-James.
They both thought the monastic
garden particularly successful.

YOICKS! OR, THE FOX OUTFOXED

Article written for *The New York Yimes,* 1949

ONE of the more enjoyable of the controversies which regularly enliven public life in England from time to time is that aroused by the proposal to abolish blood sports. With us this sanguinary term is used rather loosely to cover all forms of sport which involve the pursuit and death of animals; but it is normally confined to the hunting with hounds of foxes, stags and hares, and the coursing of hares with greyhounds.

No other subject (with the possible exceptions of corporal punishment in schools and a fixed Easter) arouses such heat or is debated with such enthusiasm and lack of restraint. The most recent of many attempts to legislate against it, a private member's bill in the House of Commons to render illegal all the above-mentioned forms of hunting, has just been defeated, but one can safely assume that the controversy is likely to continue as embittered as ever.

Few more powerful arguments with which to sustain the charge of English illogicality can be found than that provided by the national attitude toward animals. On the one hand, our dumb friends are in this country sentimentalized to a degree quite impossible anywhere else; on the other, they are hunted and slaughtered with unequalled enthusiasm. Nevertheless, even the most unreflective Nimrods seem occasionally to be aware that there is something vaguely contradictory in their outlook, and their efforts to resolve the dilemma usually take the form of explaining that no one enjoys a day out with the hounds more than the fox.

In view of the extreme difficulty of obtaining any direct evidence to the contrary, this statement is often allowed to pass unchallenged; thus no need arises to fall back on the more honest, perhaps, but less popular argument, "I enjoy a run with the hounds, so do the hounds, so whether or not the fox does, doesn't matter a tuppenny damn."

Whatever degree of blood lust enters into the enjoyment of fox hunters, it is by no means invariably the fox which satisfies it: there is always the possibility that one of the more unpopular newcomers to the neighbourhood may injure himself severely, or even break his neck, although the chances of this particular treat are more favorable at point-to-points than in the hunting field itself. But in this connection it must be remembered that while injury or sudden death, when they befall either the fox or human beings, are all part of the fun, for a horse to strain a fetlock is unmitigated disaster, and in the event of serious injury or death the emotional equivalent of full court mourning engulfs the whole field.

The popularity of fox hunting among the English does not depend exclusively on the pleasures of the

chase itself. Almost as powerful a factor is the opportunity it provides for dressing up. Now the English, one would imagine, judging by the nature of the remarks they pass on the foreigner's passion for uniforms, or the goings-on of the Elks or similar fraternities, have no great liking for fancy dress, but this is not the case.

It is only the nature of the pleasure they obtain from it that is peculiar. Whereas elsewhere sartorial rivalry finds expression in attaining a greater richness, a higher degree of fantasy than one's neighbour, in England it is the closest possible conformity to the established ideal which counts. And nowhere is it possible to indulge this passion so satisfactorily as in the hunting field; where all are dressed exactly alike such details as the tying of a stock, the exact degree of polish on a boot, the subtlest curve in the brim of a hat, take on an immense and proper significance and may cause the most jealous heartburning.

Moreover, there is always the additional pleasure of being rude to those who have failed to conform to the established pattern or have deliberately flouted it, although this is not always without its dangers. On one occasion a horrified hunt member went up to that celebrated and dandified oil magnate, Mr. Gulbenkian, on his first appearance in the field and remarked in a broken voice that in forty years' experience he had never before seen anyone come out with the Pytchley wearing an orchid, only to receive the shattering reply, "If it comes to that, my dear sir, I expect that it is the first time in forty years you've ever seen an Armenian come out with the Pytchley."

In addition to the pleasures of dressing up, there is all the satisfaction to be derived from taking part in an elaborate traditional ritual with its own language and observances. The knowledge of exactly when to shout "Tally-ho" with the full appreciation of the true

PRO—In this corner we have the fox-hunting gentry (who frequently seem as much interested in their haberdashery as they are in varmints) along with humbler types who like to dash across fields in pursuit of hounds in pursuit of hares.

significance of this mystic formula produces a feeling of well-being almost as powerful as that induced by a copious draught of sherry or cherry brandy drunk on horseback at the meet. If the meet itself is taking place, as it frequently does, in the grounds of some local nobleman's mansion, against some spreading classical façade enclosed between bare avenues of beech or elm, the whole performance takes on an aesthetic quality of a high order.

Fox hunting, although undoubtedly the blood sport which (together with stag hunting) arouses the most frenzied opposition, is by no means the only pastime involving the death of dumb animals. There is beagling, which to an outsider would seem to involve all the exertion of fox hunting without a horse to share the burden; there is otter hunting, to which opposition appears rather more rational; there is shooting, which, however deplorable an effect it may have on the moral characters of those engaged in it, few would care to see disappear in an almost meatless England, and there is coursing.

This last, although confined to a small section of the population and geographically to the north of England, has a peculiar importance politically and its popularity may well have proved the rock on which the abolitionists' efforts foundered. For unlike that of all the other blood sports, its banning could not be presented by the present government as another victory in the class war. The reason is that this form of the chase—which is cheap, since it consists solely of setting greyhounds to chase a hare and involves none of the elaborate ritual of other forms of hunting—has enthusiastic followers among miners, all of whom, it is safe to say, can be relied on to vote Labour with the same solid regularity with which fox hunters vote Tory. But nevertheless, the devotees of coursing who frequently devote all their spare time and cash to the cherishing of their dogs are as fanatically attached to their own sport as the most crusted Master of fox hounds.

And yet it is undoubtedly as open to charges of gross cruelty as any other blood sport, and any attempt to exempt it from the scope of legislation would have been too barefaced a piece of vote-catching for any administration.

Curiously enough, fishing is not regarded as a cruel sport and it is invariably exempted from all proposed bans. Although as a fisherman I am delighted, as a supposedly rational

CONTRA—The anti-blood fraternity seem to be anti a lot of other things, too. The ranks of the faithful include "vegetarians, teetotalers, survivors of the pro-Boer, Suffragette and anti-vaccination brigades—veterans of a hundred protest meetings."

human being I admit being puzzled. Fish, it is maintained, don't feel pain; a belief firmly held by many who are among the first to dismiss any allegation of the fox's keen enjoyment of the hunt as cynical sophistry. To me it would appear that, lacking the guaranteed testimony of a reliable trout, both theories are equally speculative. And, given the choice of ending my days either as a low-flying pheasant or a fresh-run salmon, I would decide for the moors every time. However, let me freely admit that such sombre reflections have never for one moment interfered with my pleasure on the banks of the Test.

The ranks of those attacking blood sports, although, perhaps, less colourful than their opponents', are far more mixed. Loud-voiced and most prominent are the professional abolitionists, veterans of a hundred protest meetings, who combine a detestation of "cruel" sports with vegetarianism, teetotalism, arts-and-crafts and the advocacy of co-education. Among them are many battle-scarred survivors of such historic groups as the Suffragettes, the pro-Boers, the anti-vaccination brigade and the friends of Republican Spain. Under their banner also march the Theosophists, Buddhists and the prophets of the Higher Thought.

The largest contingent is formed by those who, caring as little for the well-being of foxes or stags as those who hunt them, regard the whole business as an anachronistic reminder of the vanished rule of privilege and as such to be put down as quickly as possible. Admittedly a parade of the county families, mounted on several thousand pounds' worth of the finest horseflesh, toppers gleaming, hunt buttons flashing, is not a sight of which the convinced egalitarian can easily take a completely disinterested view, but it is difficult to see what harm it does the community. It keeps a lot of people quite happily employed, and if the rapidly diminishing band of those who can afford to do so elect to keep down particular vermin by the most expensive conceivable method, why should the rest of us worry?

Allied to the social opposition is the religious. In rural districts hunting was invariably tied up with the established church, and though that familiar figure in eighteenth-century· memoirs and Victorian fiction, the huntin' parson, is now, except in Ireland, practically extinct, his ghost still lingers to scare the local nonconformists into the ranks of the abolitionists.

Last come the renegades from what one may, perhaps, describe as the fox-hunting classes. Usually intellectuals, their attitude has been determined by unfortunate experiences in early youth. Bitter memories of being bolted with at a tender age, or taking a nasty toss in Five-Mile Bottom, or just the old Oedipus complex working out in the atmosphere of Horseback Hall, have bred in them an irrational loathing that becomes violently active at the sound of the first bars of "John Peel", or the distant note of a huntsman's horn.

Thus comparing the opposed forces, it would seem that the hunters were at a grave numerical disadvantage any time this issue is revived. However, this is not altogether the case, as proved again by the recent vote. Though small in numbers, they are not wholly without allies and enjoy the unexpressed sympathy of a large body of fellow-travellers. Many English, for whom no prospect would be more disagreeable than that of having to mount a horse, retain a strong emotional bias in favour of the *idea* of hunting. It is part of an imaginary England of coaching inns, Dickensian characters, rolling, well-tilled acres, "Now the Day Is Over" played at Evensong in country churches, beer which tastes like beer, thatched cottages and Georgian manor houses, which however little relation it may now have to reality, large numbers still treasure in their hearts.

Then, finally, there is a small band who consider, perhaps illogically, that it will be time enough to start worrying about our poor dumb friends when rather more has been done to discourage human beings from killing each other.

Osbert Lancaster's pocket cartoons succeed so well because they have a firmly established viewpoint, that of the English upper class. With a mixture of affection and irony, he recorded their combination of silliness, selfishness and devastating common sense. Even his animals and birds have a telling upper-class superiority.

"If you ask me, all those people who say there's no crime wave are just shutting their noses to facts." 24.3.50

"I don't rightly know, but I think it must be the opening of the International Something physical Year." 3.7.57

"The House may well feel that the Rt. Hon. gentleman is, perhaps, attaching too little weight to those imponderable symbols of inflation which still overshadow us." 13.4.67

"Now, Margery darling, we've not forgotten, have we, what happened to that other little girl who cried 'Wolf, wolf'?" 23.2.61

"Can't you recognise Pop Art when you see it?!"
28.10.65

"Mermaid." 18.12.64

"And another thing, Leofric—we should all be grateful if you would kindly stop referring to your fellow Magi as the Afro-Asian bloc!" 27.12.61

"She may seem like St. Joan to you, Sister Innocence, but she looks a lot more like La Pasionaria to me!" 16.8.69

"Did I hear the words 'hot pants'?" 11.2.71

"Fertility symbols are all very well, but if you ask me some of these drawings are straight pornography!" 6.8.71

"Only one double-entendre in the whole dam' show!" 18.12.68

"I think there can be small doubt about who—WITH God's help—is going to be Sportsclergyman of the year." 16.11.72

"Beach inspector 6-o-one calling! Quite frankly, sir, I find myself on the horns of a dilemma." 17.8.73

Strange scene in Chelsea Labour Exchange, consequent upon the Government's ruling that Artists' Model is not an essential occupation within the meaning of the Act. BY OSBERT LANCASTER.

Below, 'After Breakfast at Kelmscott'.

Opposite, drawings for a Whitbread calendar.

119

Large-scale wall paintings at the Randolf Hotel, Oxford, illustrating Max Beerbohm's story *Zuleika Dobson*

Osbert regarded himself as a cartoonist not a caricaturist, but was capable of drawing striking portraits. On the left, Evelyn Waugh, the young Nancy Mitford with her parents (adapted from a family snapshot and used as a book jacket for one of Nancy's books). On the right, Anthony Powell and Lord Kitchener. Bottom, Cyril Connolly: the point of the joke is that Connolly was notoriously slothful and slovenly, and thus unimaginable to his friends in full diplomatic rig.

"I mentioned that at one time I had been intended for the Diplomatic Service and that I had always regarded it since with some of the wistfulness he felt for literature."
C. C. Sunday Times.
28. 9. 52.

124

THE LITTLEHAMPTON SAGA

The Littlehamptons were Osbert's satirical yardstick—his most consistent means of commenting on current foibles. He began by inventing the egregious Maudie, who makes her first appearances in his *Daily Express* pocket cartoons at the end of the 1940s. Maudie is an efficient mixture of the bright and the dim. She embodies the power of the English aristocracy to adapt itself successfully to new and apparently unfavourable circumstances. She is blandly predatory, and a mistress of lateral thinking—employing this technique to her own advantage long before the term itself was invented. She is often accompanied by her husband Willie, Earl of Littlehampton, who finds the world almost completely baffling, but is as much of a born survivor as Maudie herself. There are also two horrible children who are among the few human beings who ever consistently get the better of their mother. Recognising the vitality of these creations, Osbert then provided them with an ancestry stretching back as far as the Crusades. These earlier Littlehamptons enabled him to comment (appositely) on many aspects of art and architecture: the Poet's Corner section of *Drayneflete Revealed* offers an additional glimpse of Osbert Lancaster's skill as a literary parodist.

These drawings come from *The Saracen's Head*, the earliest episode of the Littlehampton saga. The story features Sir William de Littlehampton, a distinctly reluctant Crusader, who becomes a hero in spite of himself, and his ill-behaved but faithful dog Charlemagne, who returns home minus his tail, but otherwise none the worse for his adventures.

LADY LITTLEHAMPTON AND FRIENDS
Selections from *The Littlehampton Bequest,* 1973

Of Sir Benjamin's son by his second marriage we unfortunately know little. He would seem not to have had much in common with his half-brother, spending more time at Court than in the counting-house where he soon gained a reputation as a skilled poetaster and a dexterous performer in the pavane. As a young man he spent some years in the hosuehold of the Earl of Southampton and there are those who maintain, but Dr. Rowse is not among them, that he was the original Dark Lady of the Sonnets.

He was known, at least on one occasion, to have trailed a pike in the Low Countries when there were those among his companions who loudly proclaimed that in his case 'trailed' was the operative word.

With the accession of James I his social success markedly increased and no masque was regarded as worth

Among the many carefree young gallants at the Court of King Charles I few cut so dashing a figure as Christopher de Courantsdair. High-spirited, handsome and enormously wealthy, he was equally popular with both sexes and his devotion to the House of Stuart was absolute. When the war broke out he immediately placed himself and his fortune at the disposition of his sovereign and none among the Cavaliers surpassed him in gallantry, although, it must be admitted that few displayed such tactical incompetence.

With the final defeat of the Royal cause he accompanied the Heir Apparent into exile, loyally remaining at his side until the Restoration. It is pleasant to record that his devotion did not go unrewarded; not only were his estates restored to him, but on his marriage to an old friend of the King he was created Viscount Drayneflete and made

the watching in which he did not have a prominent role, but with the onset of middle age he rapidly put on weight and his sovereign's anxiety to have him always about his person became less acute. At the same time his half-brother's reluctance to pay the debts which his personal extravagance incurred became more marked, and soon the Court revels knew him no more. He ended his days in almost total obscurity, living on the charity of his nephew. He never married.

Master of the Ordnance, and he continued high in the Royal favour until the very end of the reign. It was, perhaps, the jealousy such marked favour aroused which earned him the title of 'the Wicked Lord', for it is hard to see that he exceeded in iniquity the majority of his contemporaries. While it is just possible that the tale of his seduction of the eleven-year-old daughter of the Bishop of Barnstaple in her father's vestry may have some foundation in fact, there would seem little to justify the frequent charges of sodomy.

LOUISE, the young wife of the elderly Baron de Stellenbosch who did so much to render life tolerable for King Charles II during his exile, was said by general report to have come from an armigerous Walloon family residing in Antwerp, but there were those who declared her to be the natural daughter of the Cardinal-Archbishop of Utrecht. Whatever her origins all were agreed on her beauty and her sympathetic nature. She first met the exiled monarch under her husband's roof and a rewarding and comparatively long-standing relationship soon developed. When the King came into his own again she accompanied him to London, the Baron having tactfully died a month or two earlier, but it is sad to have to relate that their delightful intimacy did not long survive the sea-change. Yet, despite new involvements, the monarch remained ever mindful of all her kindness and saw to it that she was firmly established in a state suitable to her rank, and upon her marriage to his old friend, Sir Christopher de Courants-

WHEN Viscount Drayneflete went into exile with his sovereign he was accompanied by his younger brother Guy. A studious and, compared to his brother, unglamorous youth, he soon abandoned the Royal entourage in the Low Countries and made his way to Rome, where he not only reverted to the faith of his mother's family, but took Orders. Great was the rejoicing in Vatican circles at the return to the fold of so prominent a lost sheep, and he was soon comfortably installed in the household of Cardinal Azzolino where, it is said, he played an important part in the conversion of Queen Christina.

Amiable and hospitable, his apartments in the Palazzo Condotti became in time a place of pilgrimage for his countrymen passing through Italy, among them John Evelyn, who viewed his extremely comfortable way of life, and in particular 'a little sloe-eyed serving wench', with Protestant disapproval. While conscientious in fulfilling all his ecclesiastical duties he did not abandon those sporting

dair, the bridegroom was immediately raised to the peerage and the bride receive not only a number of very good livings but also a monopoly on the import of Dutch gin.

At Court where she immediately secured, and long retained, a prominent position, she commanded universal admiration and her charms were celebrated in the verses of Rochester and the paintings of Lely. 'To the playhouse', writes Pepys, 'where I was mightily pleased to find myself in company with my lady Drayneflete.'

diversions characteristic of an English gentleman and was reckoned the best shot in the Curia; nor did he neglect to cultivate scholarly pursuits, publishing a large folio volume, *De Gustibus Romanorum*, in which he gives no less than thirty-two different recipes for stuffing a partridge.

When in 1769 the 3rd Earl of Littlehampton was in Rome on the Grand Tour he had the curiosity to visit his great-great-uncle's lodgings which he found to be carefully preserved by a withered crone of immense age, from whom, with some difficulty, he managed to acquire this splendid bust.

AUGUSTUS de Courantsdair succeeded his father, the 1st Viscount Drayneflete, while still a child. Coming of a family devoted to the Stuarts and with an uncle at the Vatican, it might have been thought that he had a great future at Court, but his natural sagacity rendered him mistrustful of King James's chances, and in fact few of the nobility gave so enthusiastic a welcome to Dutch William. His foresight was soon rewarded and after the Battle of the Boyne, at which he arrived, a little late, at the head of his own company of horse, he was made the 1st Earl of Littlehampton of the second creation.

THE 1st Earl's marriage to the only daughter of the immensely wealthy Sir Solomon Bunbury, Bt., a Lord Mayor of London who, it was said, owned half the plantations in the West Indies, might well be described as 'à la mode', but thanks to the strength of character displayed by both parties the outcome was far removed from the dismal débâcle in which Hogarth's characters were involved. The bride, whose mother had been a Miss ffosil of Norfolk, inherited not only the beauty which had made that lady the Queen of the Swaffham Assembly Rooms but much of the energy which her grandfather had so successfully displayed in the management of his estates. In Laroon's delightful canvas she is shown in mourning for her husband, who had died the previous year, and accompanied by her two daughters, Letitia and Euphemia with, in the background, her devoted page Hasdrubal, who had been born on her father's estate in Jamaica. This engaging blackamoor was held in the highest esteem by the whole family and his mistress took a particular pleasure in his company and insisted on his being always about her person.

POET'S CORNER

Taken from *Drayneflete Revealed*, 1949

A T THE beginning of the nineteenth century the main road to the coast was practically unflanked by buildings after it crossed the river by the old bridge and a ten-minutes walk from the Market Place in this direction was sufficient to take the traveller into virgin country. A little more than a mile from the bridge there was a crossroads at which stood a single humble inn opposite the recently completed walls of Lord Littlehampton's great park. The second Earl, 'Sensibility Littlehampton' as he was known, at the time of the second rebuilding of Drayneflete Castle conceived the kindly idea of building a small Gothic Lodge at this corner of his estate for his friend and protégé, the poet Jeremy Tipple. It was the long residence of this celebrated bard in this villa which first gained for the crossroads the appellation 'Poet's Corner', and it was here that he wrote his immortal *The Contemplative Shepherd*, a poem of some fifteen thousand lines of which we can, alas, only quote a small selection. The passage chosen is of particular topographical interest as the landscape described is today almost entirely covered by the municipal sewage farm.

Th'enamelled meadows that can scarce contain
The gentle windings of the limpid Drayne
Full oft have seen me, wandering at dawn
As birds awaken and the startled fawn
Leaps from her mossy bed with easy grace
On catching sight of my indulgent face.
Deep in some crystal pool th'enamoured trout
Frolics and wantons up a lichened spout
By which the stream, in many a sparkling rill,
Is made by art to turn a water-mill.
At last the sluggard Phoebus quits his bed
And bares the glory of his fiery head;
Now all the world assumes an aspect new
And Nature blushes neath the mantling dew.
E'en yonder mossy walls and em'rald sward
The home of Littlehampton's puissant lord,
The ancient fastness of a warrior race
Regards these marches with a kindlier face. . . .

By 1820 both the poet and his patron were dead. Owing to the slump at the end of the Napoleonic Wars, coupled with a bad run of luck at Crockfords, the nephew and successor of the second Earl ('Sensibility Littlehampton' had never married) had been forced to sell land for development and a row of gentlemen's villas to the design of Mr. Papworth had been erected alongside Poet's Corner, while a bailiff's cottage in the Rustic style was erected on the further side of the inn some years later. The Gothic Villa itself was now in the possession of Miss Amelia de Vere, the only child of the poet's married sister, Sophonisba, who had long kept house for her brother. Along with the house Miss Amelia

had inherited much of her uncle's poetic gift, although at first this was only revealed to a small circle of intimate friends. After, however, the anonymous publication of her *Lines on the Late Massacre at Chios*, which sounded like a tocsin throughout Liberal Europe, her fame was assured. It is not, alas, possible, nor indeed is it probably necessary, to quote this celebrated work in full, but the two opening verses will serve to demonstrate both the fearless realism of the gentle poetess and her exceptional command of local colour, a command the more extraordinary in that she never, save for a brief visit to Tunbridge Wells, travelled more than ten miles from Drayneflete in all her life.

> O hark to the groans of the wounded and dying,
> Of the mother who casts a last lingering look
> At her infant aloft, understandably crying,
> Impaled on the spear of a Bashi Bazook.
>
> O see where the vultures are patiently wheeling
> As the scimitars flash and the yataghans thud
> On innocent victims, vainly appealing
> To dreaded Janissaries lusting for blood.

However, although Miss de Vere may have never, save in imagination, set eyes on distant parts she was afforded many a complete change of scene on her own doorstep in the course of an extraordinarily long life. The first transformation was due to the coming of the railway. In order to save a considerable diversion and the expense of building a bridge over the Drayne, the main line kept to the south bank of the river and the station was located rather more than a mile from the centre of the town, close by Poet's Corner crossroads, and the permanent way was carried over the coast road by viaduct. This development coincided with another of Lord Littlehampton's bad runs of luck at Baden-Baden (furthermore the noble Lord had suffered grievously by the repeal of the Corn Laws) and he took the opportunity of selling off all his property to the north of the railway.

The opening of the railway and the subsequent increase in importance of this hitherto unimportant suburb led to further rapid development. In 1855 the successful termination of the Crimean War was commemorated by the erection of a memorial fountain and the *Duke of York* public-house acquired a new façade. At the same time the increase in the congregation of the ancient church of Drayneflete Parva, half a mile up the hill, thanks to the recent completion of Gotha Terrace and other residential streets on what had previously been virgin fields, encouraged the churchwardens to add a spire to the somewhat squat tower.

At the time of Miss de Vere's death in 1890 the developments described above had been carried a stage further and the whole district was beginning to lose something of its hitherto exclusively residential character. The *Duke of York* was completely rebuilt in 1885,

Poet's Corner, 1800 and 1830.

Poet's Corner, 1860.

and four years later the Drayneflete Gas Company's Works were established alongside the railway to the south. The villas adjacent to Poet's Corner were gradually turned into shops, and the new streets which came into being at this time were largely built for the convenience of a lower grade of society.

The third Earl of Littlehampton dying at an advanced age in 1883, largely due to the shock sustained after a peculiarly bad run of luck at Homburg, was succeeded by his grandson, a man of simple tastes who divided his time between the family seat at Courantsdair and his Irish home at Spanielstown. In the Jubilee year he sold Drayneflete Castle for a lunatic asylum and presented the grounds to the Municipality as a public park.

On the death of Miss de Vere, Poet's Corner passed to her nephew, Mr. Casimir de Vere-Tipple, in whom the poetic gift, so constant in this remarkable family, burnt, if not with renewed vigour, certainly with a 'hard gem-like flame'. His contributions appeared regularly in *The Yellow Book*, and were published in a slim volume by the Bodley Head under the title *Samphire and Sardonyx*. Unfor-

135

tunately he did not long enjoy his property as he was forced, for private reasons, to live abroad from 1895 onwards and thenceforth resided on Capri in a charming villa where his great social gifts and exquisite hospitality will still be remembered by many visitors.

After the departure of Mr. de Vere-Tipple the Poet's Corner was let on a long lease to a firm of monumental masons. A further great change in the appearance of the neighbourhood occurred when, shortly before the 1914 war, Messrs. Pinks, the drapers, entirely rebuilt their premises and a confectioner's acquired the space between them and the Poet's Corner. The secluded quiet of this once shady nook was further interrupted by the substitution of trams for horse-buses at the turn of the century, and the subsequent increase in traffic due to the coming of the internal combustion engine.

However, the poetic tradition of the locality was not even yet extinct. On his death in 1929 Mr.

Poet's Corner, 1890.

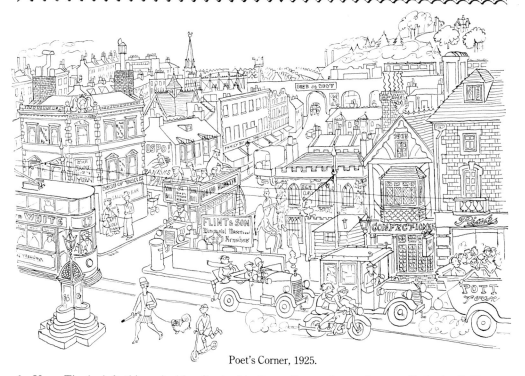

Poet's Corner, 1925.

de Vere-Tipple left this valuable site to his favourite nephew, then at Oxford, Guillaume de Vere-Tipple, who had already made a name for himself by the publication of *Feux d'artifice* (Duckworth 1927), a collection of verse astonishing in its maturity, from which we quote a single poem, *Aeneas on the Saxophone*.

> . . . Delenda est Carthago!
> (ses bains de mer, ses plâges fleuries,
> And Dido on her lilo à sa proie attachée)
>
> And shall we stroll along the front
> Chatting of this and that and listening to the band?
>
> The plumed and tufted sea responds
> Obliquely to the trombone's call
> The lecherous seaweed's phallic fronds
> Gently postulate the Fall.
>
> But between the pebble and the beach rises the doubt,
> . . . Delenda
> Between the seaside and the sea the summons,
> . . . est
> Between the *wagon* and the *lit* the implication,
> . . . Carthago.

137

In the years between the wars the whole character of the district was still further altered. In 1930 Messrs. Watlin acquired the *Duke of York*, which was at once rebuilt in a contemporary style which, although it at first struck those accustomed to the brassy vulgarity of the old "pub" as strangely austere, was soon generally agreed to be both socially and aesthetically an immense improvement. Two years later another even more daring example of "the Modern Movement", as it had come to be known, arose in the shape of the Odium Cinema. While some of the more old-fashioned residents might find fault with the functional directness of this great building, nothing but praise could be accorded to the modified Georgian style in which the new Council flats across the road were built at much the same date.

The coming of a new age, of which the buildings round Poet's Corner were a portent, found a reflection in the poet's verse. Guillaume de Vere-Tipple was socially conscious to a remarkable degree and had long entertained doubts as to the security of capitalist society, doubts which received striking confirmation when International Nickel, in which he had inherited a large holding, slumped to $11^1/2$. Making a clean break with the past, his next volume of poetry, *the liftshaft* (Faber and Faber 1937), appeared above the signature Bill Tipple, and, as may be seen from the poem quoted below, this reorientation is reflected in the contents:—

crackup in barcelona

among the bleached skeletons of the olive-trees
stirs a bitter wind
and maxi my friend from the mariahilfer strasse
importunately questions a steely sky
his eyes are two holes made by a dirty finger
in the damp blotting paper of his face
the muscular tissues stretched tautly across the scaffolding of bone
are no longer responsive to the factory siren
and never again will the glandular secretions react
to the ragtime promptings of the palais-de-danse
and I am left balanced on capricorn
the knife-edge tropic between anxiety and regret
while the racing editions are sold at the gates of football grounds
and maxi lies on a bare catalan hillside
knocked off the tram by a fascist conductor
who misinterpreted a casual glance.

The late war dealt hardly with Poet's Corner. Fortunately the house itself is still standing, but the confectioner's next door was totally demolished and extensive damage was caused to much of the surrounding property. After the end of the conflict, in a misguided effort to relieve the considerable local housing shortage, an estate of pre-fabricated dwelling-houses was erected by the Borough Council in what had been erstwhile the shady groves and green retreats of the Littlehampton Memorial Park.

Today Poet's Corner is up for sale: its owner, Bill Tipple, who on the outbreak of war had been a conscientious objector, but who, on hearing the news of the invasion of Russia, experienced a complete change of heart and immediately joined the Drayneflete section of the National Fire Service, is absent for long periods abroad in his capacity of organising secretary of the World Congress of International Poets in Defence of Peace. The long Littlehampton connection with the town is now a thing of the past; the great race of Ffidgets is extinct. But their spirit lives on and their successors on the Borough Council are determined that the Drayneflete tradition shall at all costs be maintained. But, whatever the future may hold in store, let the visitor reflect as he goes round the Museum, as he inspects the magnificent collection of Ffidget portraits in the Art Gallery (bequeathed to the town in 1948 by the late Miss Dracula Parsley-ffigett), as he wanders in the old-world Market Place, as he paces the banks of the "limpid Drayne", let him reflect on the men and women who through the ages have all played their part in making Drayneflete what it is today and see to it that we, their heirs, shall prove ourselves worthy of so goodly a heritage.

Poet's Corner, 1949.

LADY LITTLEHAMPTON AND FRIENDS

Maudie portrayed by the fashionable portraitists of her time, in the style of Picasso, Sargent and Augustus John. Overleaf, a selection of *Daily Express* cartoons depicting Maudie Littlehampton and her circle.

"It might interest you to know, Willy, darling, that there are now precisely thirty-five shopping minutes to Christmas." 24.12.57

"—and everywhere she's in rather kinky chains." 4.3.71

"Wouldn't it be wonderful if just for once in one's life one could go to a party without somebody saying: 'Après nous le déluge!'?" 14.7.50

"—And one seven-guinea bottle of Paroxysme d'Amour to darling Mummy, with love and kisses from Santa Claus—all to be charged to Lady Littlehampton's account." 23.12.50

"Would one be wrong in thinking that Trudi spent her Sunday afternoon off advocating peace?" 9.5.50

"Oh, to hell with Nancy Mitford! What I always say is—if it's ME it's U!' 1.5.56

"Maudie, help!! I've got a moth in my status symbol!" 13.6.61

"Why can't Mummy get an angry young man of her own to be exploited by?" 16.4.57

"Excuse me asking, but which side are you on—pollutionwise?" 12.5.71

HEMINGWAY CRASHES IN WILD JUNGLE

"I suppose the next think we'll hear is that Enid Blyton's been kidnapped by the fairies!" 26.1.54

"My dear Maudie, as no one in their right mind could ever conceivably consider stealing Sargent's portrait of your mother, it is wholly pointless your asking me what I would be prepared to pay to get it back!" 2.9.61

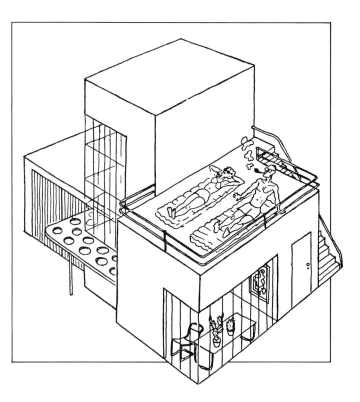

ARCHITECTURE

Osbert Lancaster invented one genre which was particularly his own—that of architectural satire. *Progress at Pelvis Bay* was his first venture. The text still has a little of the knockabout, farcical quality of purely historical parodies such as *1066 and All That. Drayneflete Revealed* is subtler, and it is not surprising that it became one of the author's most popular works. *Here, of All Places!*, which evolved and was expanded through a number of editions (the first version, then called *Homes Sweet Homes*, was published as early as 1939), shows Osbert at full stretch as an observer of both English and American architecture and domestic interiors, The nineteenth-century portion of the book shows Osbert at his most brilliant, examining and categorising material which till then had never been thought about properly, and provided labels for it which are still used today, often in a more serious fashion than their inventor intended. The lecture 'The Future of the Past' is full of good sense, and shows the foundation of deep seriousness on which Osbert built his satire.

ORDER TO VIEW

Taken from *Here of All Places,* 1958

AROUND none of the arts, with the possible exceptions of dry-fly fishing and twelve-tone music, has so formidable a mystique been woven as that which befogs architecture. From Ruskin onwards architectural writers have not hesitated either to expand their subject to cover a variety of moral and sociological themes for which the pretext was not immediately, or indeed subsequently, obvious; or else so to isolate it from the rest of human experience as to render it for the ordinary reader as remote and incomprehensible as the quantum theory. Both these attitudes are the result of an inferiority complex induced by the very nature of architecture, half art, half science. A century ago architects were hagridden by the fear lest they be thought less "creative", artistically speaking, and therefore less socially acceptable, than painters or musicians: today they are scared stiff lest they be considered less realist than engineers.

The confusion thus induced in the mind of the public seemed to me twenty years ago, when the slim volumes of which the present work is an expansion first appeared, and still seems, wholly deplorable; for with none of the arts is the layman so inescapably involved as with architecture. He is not compelled, provided he is a bachelor and can still turn a knob, to listen to Hindemith or Count Basie; it is still, just, possible to go through life without ever consciously seeing a Picasso; no compulsion as yet exists, anyhow this side of the curtain, to read Auden or buy a ticket for Sartre. But architecture is always with us; we sit in it, work in it, and pass by whole chunks of it every day. Only Red Indians and troglodytes can completely escape its unvarying pressure. My object, therefore, was twofold. First, to do for buildings what so many popular writers have done for birds, to render them a source of informed interest and lively excitement for the passer-by so that his quiet satisfaction at having identified a nice bit of Bankers' Georgian might equal that of the keen bird-watcher on having spotted a red-breasted fly-catcher; second, and with no very sanguine hopes of achievement, that such an interest, once stimulated, might become so widespread as to cause inconvenience to speculative builders, borough survey-ors, government departments and other notorious predators.

During the last two decades much has happened, at least in England, to further my purpose. The war and its aftermath enforced the realisation that while architecture might well be, as Goethe so succinctly put it, frozen music it has, nevertheless, an unfortunate tendency to melt. As the number of masterpieces, and agreeable run-of-the-mill examples, of the architecture of the past was steadily reduced by the activities first of the Luftwaffe and then of the Church Commissioners, the Ministry of Transport and other bureaucratic juggernauts, so did their value in the eyes of the public increase. At the same time a worthy eagerness, not perhaps in every case entirely unconnected with economic developments, inspired an ever-increasing number of stately-homeowners to share, on certain days, their treasures with the public at large. Furthermore the eloquence and enthusiasm of such speakers as Mr. Betjeman and Sir John Summerson brought architecture increasingly to the notice of the listening millions, and have done much to extirpate some once popular errors of taste. Thus the antiquarian heresy, first denounced by Mr. Betjeman, has lost much of its power to harm. Merit is no longer determined solely by age, and Gothic is not now invariably exalted at the expense of Georgian. And the resultant urge to put every building, no matter how contemporary its purpose, into period fancy dress is likewise on the wane.

New myths, however, have not been lacking to replace the old and to colour sound judgement. It has come to be widely believed, for instance, that some peculiar redeeming merit lies in extreme simplicity, and whereas in earlier times it was piously hoped that a bad design could be redeemed by an abundance of ill-conceived ornament it is now held for gospel that a total absence of trimmings will automatically ensure a good one. The Keatsian confusion of truth and beauty is more widespread than ever, so that while the architectural merits (such as they are) of Michelangelo's dome are briskly discounted on the grounds that the whole thing is held together by a concealed chain, unstinted praise is accorded some dreary office block solely on the grounds that its supremely uninteresting method of construction is clearly apparent to every casual passer-by. Functionalism, that arose as an understandable and, in the main, praiseworthy reaction against nineteenth-century architectural fancy dress, has been exalted into a dogma so that now nothing is ever left to our imagination and we are all forced, whether we want to or not, to watch the dullest conceivable wheels go round. Enlightened public opinion, it is clear, is not yet so powerful that either architects or their patrons can with any safety be left unwatched for more than a few seconds.

Nevertheless my primary purpose is neither didactic nor propagandist. The present expanded volume remains like its predecessors "primarily a picture-book and the letter-press is intended to do no more than provide a small mass of information leavened by a large dose of personal prejudice". In the twenty years that have elapsed since these words were written I am all too conscious of having grown much older but have no confidence at all that I am become any the wiser, so that youthful prejudices have been left unaltered even though they have in some cases been modified or flatly contradicted by those acquired in middle age. Thus I no longer find nineteenth-century Gothic so invariably funny as once I did and knowledge has only served to increase my admiration for such men as Butterfield, Pearson and H. H. Richardson. Ruskin I hold to be a far finer (although still infinitely dangerous) writer than the casual references to him in the present work might lead the reader to suspect. And age has brought increased appreciation of many works both in the Perpendicular and the Elizabethan styles. On the other hand closer acquaintance has reinforced the opinion that it is very lucky for the Romans that the majority of their buildings are only known to us in an advanced state of ruin.

In one respect, however, the years have undeniably brought increase of knowledge. When *Pillar to Post* first appeared American architecture, even that of the Eastern seaboard, was for me, as it has remained for the majority of my fellow-countrymen, *terra incognita*. The nodding acquaintance subsequently acquired, brief and inadequate as it has been, is still sufficient to encourage me to some small attempt to fill the gap, and most of the fresh material in the present volume was conceived with this purpose.

To the English reader two things about American architecture may well come as a surprise, as indeed they did to the author: first, that there is so much of it, particularly of the eighteenth and early nineteenth centuries, and in most cases so well preserved; and, second, that it is, even of the earliest period, so subtly but yet so unequivocally different. This realisation, although chastening, is long overdue.

To the American the treatment by a foreigner of a subject with which he may be pardoned for considering himself already sufficiently familiar may perhaps be justified on the grounds that the national attitude, in this respect, or so it seems to me, occasionally errs on the side of insufficient appreciation. Overawed by the lofty pretensions of the innumerable *kunstforcher* who have come to roost on his shores his response to architecture is too often coloured by a high seriousness that excludes from his consideration, as in some way unworthy, some of the less pretentious of his country's buildings.

For architecture, it cannot be said too often, is not confined to temples, palaces, state capitols, churches and public libraries; the term extends, and with equal force, to drugstores, tram-depots, comfort stations and saloons. (The fact that so many of the latter do not, in fact, qualify as architecture results not from their function but their design.) And as it is in architecture that the surest, if still uncertain, guide to the character and achievements of extinct civilisations is to be found, so the testimony of these despised and unconsidered structures is likely to carry as much weight with future generations as that of more pompous and generally acclaimed undertakings. "Time which antiquates Antiquities, and hath an art to make dust of all things, hath yet spared these minor monuments." Scholars two millennia hence are as likely to base their speculations on the remains of Jo's Diner as on the ruins of Grant's Tomb.

Equally, architecture is not to be confined solely to exteriors, for the distinction drawn between it and interior decoration is arbitrary and inexact. The living-room, whether cathedral-ceilinged, open-planned or just plain cosy is as much architecture as the façade and for this reason I have not hesitated to include comparative studies of interiors. Apart from what one hopes is their intrinsic interest their inclusion seemed to me to be justified on the grounds that they might perhaps serve to humanise the whole subject and to reinforce the lesson that architecture does not exist, and is not to be studied, in a vacuum; that its full significance is only to be appreciated in relation to the daily life, the aspirations and the ideals of those it was created to shelter or amuse.

For it is not, like orchids or skiing, of its very nature exotic in all but a few climatically favoured localities, and while it is true that many of its greatest achievements adorn such well-publicised sites as the Acropolis or the Bosphorus or the Ile de France, it is subject to no geographical limitations and flourishes, or could flourish, equally well right here.

MUNICIPAL GOTHIC In these years" (1850–1870), as Mr. Guedalla informs us, "a noble impulse among architects was covering England with reproductions of the medieval antique, of which the Law Courts are the stateliest, the Randolph Hotel at Oxford not the least worthy example." By the middle of the nineteenth century the Gothic Revival had ceased to be a joke; the driving force behind it had changed from fashionable whimsy to an evangelical (the word is used in no narrow denominational sense) fervour. The Gothic was now regarded not merely as the most beautiful method of building but also the most True; a practical demonstration of the permanent validity of Keats' celebrated definition of aesthetic worth. It was a shrewd move on the part of the poet to inform us, albeit rather tartly, that the interchangeability of Truth and Beauty "is all we need

to know", for despite the gallant efforts of Mr. Ruskin, embodied in a score of thick volumes, the precise reason why any one style of building should be truer than another remains impenetrably obscure.

The revivalists, however, were not burdened with overmuch intellectual curiosity, and taking the poet at his word forged ahead, creating for posterity a noble legacy of schools, town halls and railway termini all in the purest style of the thirteenth and fourteenth centuries. At first they had confined themselves largely to ecclesiastical buildings, but had soon come to the conclusion that what was good enough for God was good enough for Caesar and in less than no time half the public buildings in the country were enriched by a splendid abundance of crockets and gargoyles, *meurtrières* and encaustic tiling.

To a lay observer it might seem that one of the principal objections to the revival of the Gothic style lay in the fact that it had evolved under conditions which found no parallel in the modern world, but in practice this objection was found to be invalid. Indeed, its greatest merit in the eyes of the architect of the period lay in its splendid adaptability, and when Sir Gilbert Scott's plan for a Gothic Foreign Office had to be abandoned owing to the unenlightened attitude of Lord Palmerston he was able by a few strokes of the pen to transform it into St. Pancras Railway Station.

GOTHIC REVIVAL II While the more ambitious nineteenth-century manifestations of the Gothic spirit in archi-

tecture may, with very few exceptions, be dismissed as deplorable, certain of the minor achievements still retain a vague period charm. In particular some of the smaller country railway stations represent a most unexpectedly successful outcome of a brave, but admittedly uncalled-for, attempt to adapt the methods of building, popular in ecclesiastical circles in the fourteenth century, to the needs of the machine age. Their merits, it must be admitted, have very little connection with architecture, but nevertheless they frequently achieve an air of cosy whimsicality not out of keeping with the spirit of our British Railways. Moreover, it cannot be denied that up till the present none of the Railway Companies (with the honourable exception of London Transport) have evolved a style for this particular type of building that is not equally inconvenient and twice as offensive.

Another branch of architecture in which this unpretentious form of Gothicism operated, with, alas, considerably less success, was the erection of public conveniences. These necessary and useful reminders of the limitations of humanity present a difficult problem for the architect; no one wishes that they shall be overwhelmingly conspicuous, but on the other hand they would belie their name were they too cunningly concealed.

The Gothic revivalists' gallant attempt to combine modesty with prominence by erecting small-scale models of fourteenth-century baptisteries in cast-iron and equipping them with the necessary plumbing was not, however, a solution to the problem that entitles them to any praise save on the score of ingenuity.

KENSINGTON ITALIANATE Although the Gothic Revival was making rapid headway throughout the early years of Queen Victoria's reign it did not attain to its greatest popularity until the sixties and seventies, and while an ever-increasing number of churches and town halls were erected in that style, domestic architecture remained for a long time unaffected. Thus when the great expansion of London during the forties and fifties led to the development of Belgravia, Paddington and Kensington, the terraces and squares which were erected in these districts were built in a style which, despite a certain monotony and, according to modern standards, considerable inconvenience, did nevertheless represent the last expiring flicker of the great classic tradition of English architecture. Although the detail was usually inferior to that of the best Regency work and the remarkable inventiveness of that style was lacking, Kensington Italianate at its best, e.g. Eaton Square, did achieve dignity and even a certain magnificence. And even when, as has happened in North Kensington and elsewhere, whole streets and terraces intended for prosperous stockbrokers have sunk to the slum-level, they still retain some faint atmosphere of shabby grandeur. (The ability to survive drastic social reverses forms an acid test for architecture and one which it can be confidently said that the arterial housing estates, the slums of the future, will certainly not be capable of satisfying.)

However, despite the impressive effect of the façades, houses built in the Kensington Italianate possessed numerous defects, such as airless and pitch-dark basements and far too many and too steep stairs. In addition, in order to create the full architectural effect intended by the builder it is necessary that all the houses in a block or terrace should receive a coat of stucco of the same colour and at the same time; a condition which the sturdy individualism of the average British householder has always rendered impossible of fulfilment. Nevertheless, their total disappearance, which seems to be merely a matter of time, will deprive London of much of its character, which the luxury flats and cosy little maisonettes in Architectural Association Georgian, which are already taking their place in Paddington, will do nothing to restore.

EARLY VICTORIAN The early Victorian or, as some purists prefer to call it, the Adelaide style, while it undoubtedly marks a decline (the elegance of the Georgian and the vitality of the Regency have both departed), nevertheless represents not unworthily the last phase of a great tradition. The lines are heavier, the decoration coarser, yet the proportions are still good and there is a general atmosphere of solidity and comfort. Painted walls now vanish, not to reappear for nearly a century, beneath a variety of patterned papers, striped, spotted and flowered. Mahogany reigns almost supreme as the popular wood for furniture, though both birch and rosewood maintain a certain vogue. Carpets are either elaborately floral in pink and white or severely patterned in billiard-cloth green or scarlet. Fireplaces are comparatively plain in marble.

However, it is not so much the quality of the individual furnishings that has altered but the quantity. Now for the first time the part tends to become more important than the whole and the room assumes the function of a museum of *objets d'art*. The mantelpiece is transformed into a parade ground for the perpetual marshalling of rows of Bristol glass candlesticks, Sèvres vases, Bohemian lustres around the glass-protected focal point of a massively allegorical clock. For the better display of whole cavalry divisions of plunging bronze equestrians, Covent Gardens of wax fruit, bales of Berlin woolwork, the drawing-room,

the library and the boudoir are forced to accommodate innumerable cupboards, consoles and occasional tables. The large family portrait loses none of its popularity but the fashion for miniatures and silhouettes enables the range of visible reminders of the importance of family ties to be extended to the third and fourth generation of uncles, aunts and cousins of every degree.

Futile as such generalisations invariably are, one may perhaps hazard a suggestion that nothing so markedly distinguished the average Victorian from other generations as this passion for tangible evidence of past emotions; a longing to recapture in some concrete form the pleasure of a visit to Carlsbad or Margate, the unbearable poignancy of Aunt Sophia's death-bed. Hence the unbounded popularity of the memento, the *Reiseandenken*, and the keepsake. Harmless and rather touching as such a fashion may be, the intrusion of this aggressively personal note into decoration led to future trouble when it became necessary to find without fail a prominent place for such a surrealist variety of objects as a sand-filled paper-weight from Alum Bay, a lock of little Willy's hair and dear Fido, stuffed and mounted.

SALUBRIOUS DWELLINGS FOR THE
INDUSTRIOUS ARTISAN While the Victorian architects were busy erecting tasteful reproductions of Chartres cathedral and the belfry of Bruges (so useful for factory chimneys) and covering the rather inefficiently drained marshes on the outskirts of Westminster with the stucco palaces of the nobility and gentry, it must not be imagined that the needs of the humbler classes of the community were in any way overlooked. In all the great new towns of the Midlands and the Industrial North large housing estates sprang up on which, by the exercise of remarkable forethought and ingenuity, so great was the anxiety lest the worker should be too far removed from the sights and sounds of the factory or mine which was the scene of his cheerful labour, a quite fantastic number of working families were accommodated. In order that the inhabitants might have the privilege of contemplating, almost ceaselessly, the visible tokens of nineteenth-century man's final triumph over nature, many of these estates were carefully built alongside the permanent way, or even, if there was a viaduct handy, actually underneath it. That the humble householders might recall the country villages from which so many of them had come, the streets were considerately left unpaved and the drainage system was made to conform to the primitive rustic models to which they were accustomed. It is true that it was found impossible to avoid a certain monotony but this was counteracted by carefully refraining from doing anything to interfere with the effects of the elements, and allowing the weather full opportunity to produce a fascinating variety of surface texture.

VICTORIAN DINING-ROOM While the drawing-room, boudoir and bedroom of the average Victorian house might from time to time undergo the most extraordinary metamorphoses, the dining-room retained almost unaltered the character it had acquired at the very beginning of the period until, in many cases, the war of 1914. It seems as though the Victorians while willing to tolerate frivolous decorative experiments in those less important apartments were not for one moment prepared to allow any light-hearted tampering with a shrine sacred to the important processes of mastication and digestion. Moreover, not only was the dining-room safe from purely temporal changes but also from those arising from personal idiosyncrasies so that its form and decoration were practically standardised throughout the upper and middle classes.

The table, sideboard and chairs were invariably of mahogany and of a sufficiently massive construction safely to support the respective weights of the serried rows of decanters and side dishes, the monumental *épergnes* and the diners themselves. The wallpaper was always dark and nine times out of ten of a self-patterned crimson design; that colour being considered, quite rightly, as stimulating to the appetite. The carpet was invariably a fine Turkey.

Conventions no less rigid governed the choice of pictures. These, if they were not ancestral portraits, had either to be still-lives or landscapes and in both cases the choice of subject was sternly restricted. If they were still-lives they must be those vast pyramids of foodstuffs in which the red of the lobster strikes so bold a note of colour, beloved of the Dutch School, if landscapes, then storms at sea, Highland cattle or forests of a fearful gloom. (The only permissible exceptions to this depressing range were scenes in the Holy Land and then only if depicted at sunset.) Late in the period conversation pieces were allowed provided the personnel were carousing Cardinals. Generally speaking the only alternative to oil-paintings as a form of wall decoration were steel engravings, preferably by Mons. Doré, of sacred subjects. (It should never be forgotten that the dining-room of the period had taken over some of the functions of a private chapel in that it was invariably the scene of family prayers.)

So lasting were these traditions that the childhood memories of many still comparatively young retain their ineffaceable impress. Thus the sight of a Van der Velde seascape still brings the taste of mulligatawny whistling up from the author's subconscious while the flavour of Bordeaux pigeon summons with all the completeness of Proust's tea-soaked madeleine an unforgettable cloud of Mons. Doré's angels hovering over the Colosseum.

PUBLIC-HOUSE CLASSIC In the earlier part of the nineteenth century it was assumed, and rightly, that a little healthy vulgarity and full-blooded ostentation were not out of place in the architecture and decoration of a public-house, and it was during this period that the tradition governing the appearance of the English pub was evolved. While the main body of the building conformed to the rules governing South Kensington Italianate, it was always enlivened by the addition of a number of decorative adjuncts which, though similar in general form, displayed an endless and fascinating variety of treatment. Of these the most important was the plate-glass window which took up a large section of the façade, and was invariably made the excuse for a virtuoso display of decorative engraving in which may frequently be detected the ingenuous working of a native taste for the Baroque that nowadays can only find expression in the decoration of merry-go-rounds and cigar-boxes. Hardly less important were the enormous lantern which was suspended from an equally imposing and lavishly decorated curlicue at the corner of the building, the whole forming a triumph of nineteenth-century ironwork, and the splendid and elaborate examples of the sign-writer's art with which the façade was always generously enlivened.

But, alas, with the spread of popular education even the brewers became cultured and the typical pub, such as the one illustrated here, gave way to every variety of Gothic hostelry and its homely façade was soon hidden behind a copious enrichment of coloured brickwork and encaustic tiles. Says Ruskin sadly, writing in 1872, "there is scarcely a public-house near the Crystal Palace but sells its gin-and-bitters under pseudo-Venetian capitals copied from the church of the Madonna of Health or of Miracles."

But worse was still to come. Half-baked culture was succeeded by a poisonous refinement which found expression in olde worlde half-timbering and a general atmosphere of cottagey cheeriness. Fortunately a number of the old-fashioned pubs still survive in the less fashionable quarters, but the majority of them are doubtless doomed and will shortly be replaced by tasteful erections in the By-Pass Elizabethan or Brewers' Georgian styles.

LE STYLE ROTHSCHILD The Victorian passion for symbols, so essentially charming and domestic in its origins, soon proved capable of considerable expansion. If room could be found for an endless collection of objects whose sole justification was sentimental, then there was ample accommodation available for concrete reminders, not of happy moments of the householder's past, but of the satisfactory state of his financial present. *Objets d'art et de vertu* had been collected by rich men since the beginning of the seventeenth century, but, in the majority of cases, for their own sake; now they are feverishly sought after for the kudos they acquire for their owners and as visible evidence of enormous wealth. In order properly to display these hoards of Dutch pictures, Italian marbles, German glass and what-have-you, a style was evolved which combined all the richest elements of those which had preceded it and which soon became standardised throughout Europe. The heavy golden cornices, the damask-hung walls, the fringed and tasselled curtains of Genoese velvet, the marble and the parquet were as rich and as inevitable in the wealthiest circles of Vienna as they were in London, and formed almost the official background for the flashy pageant of the Second Empire.

Nothing in this style, which we have named Rothschild after what was, until recently, its finest existing example in this country—the old Rothschild house in Piccadilly—was new save the gasoliers: and the only original element was a fondness for the recent past which displayed itself in a taste for the more lavishly gilded examples of Louis Quinze furniture (hitherto each succeeding generation had surveyed the styles of its predecessors with the utmost distaste and when Empire furniture came in Chippendale went out to join the Sheraton and the Queen Anne in the servants' hall). Nevertheless, despite this ample evidence of cultural insufficiency, one is forced to admit, if like Henry James one "can stand a lot of gilt", that it was a style that at least possessed the courage of its opulent convictions. As such it flourished exceedingly on the other side of the Atlantic where it was ideally attuned to the rugged individualism of the age of the Robber Barons.

SCOTTISH BARONIAL Whatever may be said in favour of the Victorians," remarks Mr. P. G. Wodehouse, "it is pretty generally admitted that few of them were to be trusted within reach of a trowel and a pile of bricks." The sage when he made this profound observation was thinking of the English country house of the period; had he been referring to a similar building of the same date north of the Border it is probable that he would have expressed himself even more forcibly. For awe-inspiring as were the results of the archaeological enthusiasm and light-hearted fantasy of Victorian architects working in England, these worthies seem frequently to have reserved the most ambitious efforts of their breathtaking virtuosity for the benefit of their Scottish patrons.

In a praiseworthy attempt to provide the Northern kingdom with an ample supply of stately homes, they evolved a style which they hoped adequately symbolised the rugged virtues and lurking romance of the inhabitants of

> Caledonia stern and wild
> Meet nurse for a poetic child

and which they christened Scottish Baronial. It was, as the name implies, essentially an upper-class style and one which mirrored faithfully that passion on the part of the nobility and gentry for combining the minimum of comfort with the maximum of expense that has always exercised so great an influence over our domestic architecture. Spiral staircases of a steepness and gloom that rendered oubliettes unnecessary; small windows which made up for the amount of light they kept out by the amount of wind they let in; drains which conformed to medieval standards with an accuracy which in the rest of the structure remained an eagerly desired but as yet unattained ideal. These were among the invariable features of the style, but were looked on as but a small price to pay for the impressive silhouette, the battlements, the corbels and cloud-piercing turrets of the granite-laden exterior. Moreover, if the Dear Queen could not only endure but actually welcome these little inconveniences inseparable from a truly baronial existence in the Highlands, how could lesser mortals complain if they cracked their skulls on the old-world groining in the Baron's privy or caught pneumonia from the bracing wind that whistled so romantically through the latticed windows of the brand-new keep?

Although the Scottish Baronial was primarily a domestic style, it is interesting to note that it was also extensively employed for prisons.

The official religion of Victorian England is usually considered to have been an evangelical form of Christianity suitably modified to bring it into harmony with a public school education and the principles of free trade, but one is sometimes tempted to wonder whether in large tracts of the country, particularly in Scotland, an older faith that

blended ancestor worship with totemism did not reassert its hold on the upper class from about the fifties onwards. How else can we explain the sudden appearance of those vast, castellated barracks faithfully mimicking all the least attractive features of the English home at the most uncomfortable period of its development,

and filled with rank upon rank of grim-visaged, elaborately kilted forebears? What other explanation can be found for the presence of these enormous necropolitan menageries stuffed full of stags and caribou, bears and tigers—creatures which, however attractive in life, in death perform no function but the constant employment of legions of housemaids with dusters? What other reason can be advanced for the phenomenal popularity of Mr. Landseer whose only merit as a painter was the tireless accuracy with which he recorded the more revoltingly sentimental aspects of the woollier mammals?

Whether or not Scottish Baronial has its origins in primitive religion its popularity was soon assured in all classes of society. Tartan, stags' heads and faithful representations of Highland cattle in various media soon enlivened the Coburg simplicity of the Court as successfully as they added to the discomfort of cosy little villas in Tulse Hill or Twickenham where the rafters were unlikely ever to ring with the sound of the pipes. And today many a dusty hotel lounge, many a dentist's waiting-room with their ritual display of these old symbols, recall, like the mosques of Spain, the former domination of a vanished faith.

ACCOMMODATION

Taken from *Progress at Pelvis Bay,* 1936

THE evolution of the great modern luxury hotel from its humble beginnings as a wayside inn is one of the most fascinating phenomena of recent times and nowhere can it be studied to greater advantage than at Pelvis Bay. By the courtesy of the proprietors of the Ship Hotel, I am able to publish a remarkable series of pictures which show in the clearest possible way, and in considerable detail, the various stages through which this historic hostelry has passed. When Pelvis Bay was still a poverty-stricken collection of fishermen's huts it could only boast one tavern, the Ship, a wretched weather-boarded cottage on the quay. While this doubtless proved quite adequate for the needs of the simple fisherfolk it was in no way capable of satisfying the more exigeant requirements of the summer visitors. However, as at first the majority of these preferred to rent apartments rather than to stay in an hotel, and as the proprietor of the inn lacked both the capital and the initiative to expand, it was not until the house had been acquired by a syndicate at the time of the coming of the railway that it was decided to rebuild.

Once this decision had been arrived at the work was immediately put into the best possible hands; namely, those of Sir Septimus Ogive. He was given carte blanche and assured that no expense would be spared to make this the finest hotel in Europe and an example of what a great modern hotel could and should be. The style decided upon was thirteenth-century Flemish-East Anglian and this was rigidly kept to throughout, even such small details as the fire-screens and the gasoliers being personally designed by the architect.

The result was almost miraculous and immediately evoked the most widespread admiration. In fact it was confidently stated by contemporary critics that for purity of design there were only three buildings of the same period in the country that could even approach it: the Randolph Hotel at Oxford, the Angel Choir at Lincoln and the St. Pancras Railway Station. Many famous figures of the Victorian Age were at one time or another visitors to this hotel, and many of them have left eloquent tokens of their appreciation in the historic visitors' book. Thus we find after Mr. Ruskin's name the following beautiful compliment: "Not only is the water hot but the bathroom has a Moral Beauty of its own in no way connected with its mere utilitarian value." Two or three pages later we find Alfred (not then Lord) Tennyson starting a complaint as to the condition in which his shirts have returned from the laundry with the witty comment, "Tears, idle tears, I know not what they mean!" In the manager's office is still preserved a letter from Dickens pointing out

1870

1902

that the boot-boy had gone off with his trousers, a laughable incident that the great man himself was the first to appreciate.

However, despite a natural reluctance on the part of the management to change these almost hallowed surroundings it was decided at the time of the accession of King Edward VII, much to the understandable annoyance of Sir Septimus, that the time had come to redecorate the hotel throughout and to adopt various modern improvements. While the interior was completely renovated, the greatest care was taken that the celebrated façade should in no way be altered. Electric lighting, a passenger lift and numerous additional bathrooms were installed, and all the public rooms were done up in the style of Louis-Seize. The effect was, at the time, generally admired, recalling, as a contemporary newspaper happily phrased it, "memories of the gracious days of the *ancien régime*, when powdered *beaux* paid their court to the beauties of Versailles in the fairy-like surroundings of the Petit Trianon."

In architectural circles the liveliest satisfaction was felt by all, that the management had had no truck with the Art Nouveau Movement, then at the height of its short-lived popularity.

This scheme of decoration remained unchanged until after the war, when it was felt that perhaps the time had come to make a change. The stately and slightly austere character of the Edwardian *décor* was considered to be rather out of keeping with the increased tempo of the machine age, and so it was decided to convert the interior into an old-world Tudor Hall. This, of course, involved extensive structural alterations of which the most important was the removal of the twin Corinthian pillars in the entrance hall and the subsequent underpinning of the roof. So skilfully was this carried out and so great was the care taken to ensure that no modern feature should occur to interfere with the illusion of antiquity, that few visitors to the hotel were ever remotely aware that the age-old beams above their heads were in reality solid pressed steel carefully grained and varnished!

So great, however, is the pace of modern life that in a very few years the management, in pursuance of their well-known policy of always keeping abreast of the times, determined once more to redecorate their premises. In 1929, when so much alteration and rebuilding were going on all over the town, they built the new Chinese Grill Room on the front and the following year called in a well-known firm of Mayfair decorators to transform the rest of the hotel. The keynote of the scheme of decoration adopted was that of a ship, and every effort was made to emphasise this nautical idea in all the details of the furnishing, with such successful results that the illusion of being on shipboard is almost complete and is only slightly impaired by the uninterrupted view of the sea obtainable from most of the windows; were it invisible there would be nothing to indicate that one was not on the most modern of transatlantic liners.

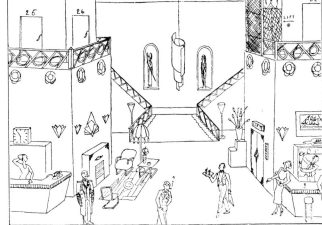

PLACES OF WORSHIP

Taken from *Progress at Pelvis Bay,* 1936

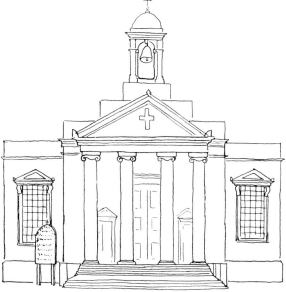

The Church of St. Paul

WHEN Pelvis Bay was still nothing but a collection of fishermen's huts, the nearest church was that of St. Pancras at Pelvis Magna, three miles inland. The simple devotion of the hardy fisherfolk made light of this six-mile tramp every Sunday, but it was not to be expected that the new annual visitors, many of whom were in delicate health, would not soon feel the want of some place of worship a little closer at hand. Moreover, its distance from the town was not the only disadvantage attaching to the old parish church; for during the earlier part of the century the incumbent, the Rev. Augustus Cinqbois, Sir Ossian's brother, could not be said in any way to share in that quickening of the nation's religious life that was such a feature of the period. He was, perhaps, although fundamentally a most God-fearing man, rather too typical a product of the eighteenth century, and his habit of conducting the service in full hunting kit and his remarkable capacity for port did little to endear him to either Evangelicals or Tractarians. So it was decided to erect a church in the town itself and the work was entrusted to a prominent London architect, and the consecration took place in 1835. It was perhaps a little unfortunate that the church of St. Paul was built when it was, for, despite a great deal of local opposition

St. James-the-Least.

and the spirited protests of the Camden Society, the style chosen was that degraded classical that was even then fast losing ground. As it was, the town had to wait another thirty years for a church that was acceptable to those who agreed with the present Bishop of London in thinking no church is a proper church "that has not a spire pointing a finger to God", as His Lordship so aptly puts it. Luckily St. Paul's is no longer standing to reproach the town with its former lack of taste as last year it was pulled down and the site disposed of by the Ecclesiastical Authorities to a prominent film combine who are this year opening a magnificent cinema, the Damascus, on the site.

The new church of St. James-the-Least, when it was finally opened in the late sixties, was universally admitted to have been well worth waiting for. Built in the Early Perpendicular style it also managed cleverly to incorporate several elements of

157

both Flemish and Venetian Gothic of the best periods. The architect was Sir Septimus Ogive (a friend and pupil of the celebrated Sir Gilbert Scott) who was a resident of Pelvis Bay for many years and recently died there at the advanced age of a hundred and two, and is buried in the shadow of what is generally considered his masterpiece. This remarkable veteran was active and true to his principles to the end, and indeed his death was generally attributed to a fit of apoplexy caused by his justifiable annoyance at the incomprehensible rejection by the county council of his plans for an Early English airport. The spire of this remarkable

The Strict Baptist Chapel.

church is one of the highest in the south of England and is a landmark for miles around and visible far out at sea. The interior is no less remarkable, and no visitor to Pelvis Bay should fail to pay it a visit. Lack of space forbids me to enumerate the various artistic treasures it contains and I must content myself with drawing attention to some of the finest. The beautiful East Window in which the story of St. Philip and the Ethiopian eunuch is portrayed in glowing colours was put up in 1902 as a memorial to two members of the congregation who spent their lives in the mission field in Abyssinia. The beautiful marble font, decorated with the Passage over Jordan in bas-relief, the work of a well-known local sculptress, was the gift of Sir Mordecai Cinqbois (né Finkelstein) on his baptism. The lovely alabaster reredos, with a pattern of water-lilies in lapis-lazuli inlay, was given to the church in 1905 by an anonymous donor and is generally considered to be one of the masterpieces of l'Art Nouveau in this country. The encaustic tiles in the main aisle are another treasure that the visitor should be careful not to overlook, as in point of colour they are not surpassed, in Professor Betjeman's opinion, by any of this date in the whole of England.

However, the C. of E., though foremost, was not alone in providing the town with fine specimens of modern ecclesiastical architecture. The Baptists, the Methodists, both primitive and ordinary, the Seventh Day Adventists, the Plymouth Brethren and even the Irvingites have all at one time or another established places of worship in the town, of which the Strict Baptist chapel in the Station Road, a thirteenth-century Gothic building in

The Church of Christ Scientist.

Sussex Flint, is perhaps the most notable (see illustration). The R.C.s have the church of St. Philip Neri, a building whose beauty of design renders the spectator almost oblivious to the somewhat harsh appearance of the corrugated iron in which it is built. The most recent addition to this list is perhaps also the finest, namely the one hundred and twenty-second Church of Christ Scientist in Campbell-Bannerman Terrace. It is a magnificent red-brick structure built in the Romanesque style. It cost one hundred and twenty thousand pounds to build, and the interior is adorned with a remarkable series of mosaics depicting scenes from the life of Mrs. Eddy.

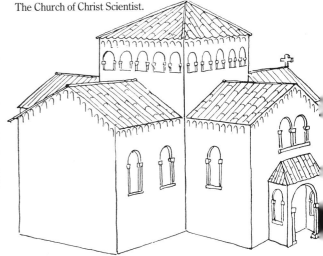

THE FUTURE OF THE PAST

Article written for *Cornhill Magazine*, 1965

THE relatively restricted areas of the globe's land surface which are generally considered habitable are today littered with a vast accumulation of architectural debris—dolmens and split-levels, basilicas and railway stations, ziggurats and manor houses. During most of recorded history the attitude of the inhabitants towards buildings put up by their predecessors was straightforward and strictly utilitarian; when these were still usable they were used, and when fallen into decay, unless protected by sanctity or taboo, unhesitatingly quarried to provide material for the erection of structures better adjusted to contemporary requirements, or more in accordance with contemporary taste. But some 200 or so years ago this robust, unsentimental approach was seriously modified by a change of feeling towards the past, of which Gibbon's musings in the Forum and Stukeley's speculations at Stonehenge are equally, although diversely, indicative. If, it was asked, monuments of ancient architecture could excite emotions at once so awesome and so agreeable—could afford if properly studied such valuable aid to the understanding of history—had they not better be carefully preserved? It is to the affirmative, if delayed, response to this query, that we owe the existence of the Society for the Protection of Ancient Buildings, the National Trust, the Georgian Group, Les Monuments Historiques, Colonial Williamsburg, Urban Renewal, and even the Association for the Preservation of Disused Branch-Line Railway Stations.

Hitherto, these and many bodies involved in what has recently, and perhaps unfortunately, come to be called "preservationism", have all enjoyed, in varying degrees, support and encouragement; but now with the ever-increasing pressure of "development" and the population explosion just around the corner, the time has come, or so it seems to me, not necessarily to limit the support, but certainly carefully to consider exactly what it is we are encouraging, and why.

Such an enquiry must of necessity be twofold: first there is the question of what we should preserve, and second of how we should preserve it.

When a building has survived its original functional usefulness – but first let us be quite sure that it has; for we all know of cases of cottages or brownstones which could be rendered perfectly comfortable at a quarter the cost of a new semi-detached or apartment house, which are yet ruthlessly swept away in the name of economy—then there are three grounds, and only three, on which we are logically entitled to press for its preservation: that of its own intrinsic aesthetic merit, that of piety, that of its scenic usefulness.

Of these it is the first upon which agreement is most difficult to reach. For no yardstick of aesthetic judgement is of universal validity; time and distance both produce the strangest reversals. No educated person would today contemplate the destruction of Chartres with equanimity, but in the eighteenth century many would have regarded it as a welcome deliverance too long delayed. And can we be certain that the obvious necessity for preserving the temple of Paestum would be self-evident to one brought up in the shadow of the Angkor Wat?

However, the consciousness that all judgements on such matters are relative does not absolve us from making them. Moreover, we are now, thanks largely to cheap printing and

photography—which, as Monsieur André Malraux has so brilliantly shown in *La Musée Imaginaire*, have widened our sensibility to almost universal dimensions—in a far better position than ever before to reach some measure of agreement. At least on works of reasonable antiquity; to those of the last 150 years individual reactions will continue to be unpredictable. Perfect harmony of views on the preservation of, say, a church by Street or H. H. Richardson is unlikely to be achieved by Dr. Gropius and Mr. Betjeman, and while many regarded Charles Rennie Mackintosh's tearooms as the fairest jewel in Glasgow's crown, and the vital link between Art Nouveau and the Modern Movement, their disappearance left others comparatively unmoved. First, then, we must bear in mind that there are degrees of value, and economic necessity frequently imposes a choice. Therefore before we set up a howl in defence of some admirable but far from unique group of cottages or a small plantation house, let us always reflect whether or not our action is going to prejudice our chances of stopping the demolition of some acknowledged masterpiece threatened at a later date. Second, let us always beware of the uncertainty of private judgement, remembering that what to us may be without merit may well prove to posterity, who can view it in perspective, of considerable value. Thirdly, the antiquarian heresy is by no means dead, and the confusion between antiquity and merit is still a common enough threat to sound judgement.

On the second ground for appeal–that of piety – a far greater measure of agreement is likely in most cases to be attained. By piety I mean, in its application to architecture, an emotion widely diffused, unaesthetic and comprehensible only in the light of a people's proper consciousness of their past. In many cases, perhaps, the buildings which evoke it will justify their continued existence also on aesthetic grounds, but not always. Take, for instance, the Tower of London or Paul Revere's house in Boston. To a detached view the former is simply an injudiciously restored, rather provincial example of twelfth-century functionalism, less offensive than the power station across the way because smaller and unselfconscious; the latter an easily matched example of colonial domestic building. But nevertheless, any threat to either would arouse a nationwide storm of righteous indignation. Such a reaction is in my view right and proper; and, responding to some of the deepest feelings of the human race, is not to be dismissed as pure sentimentality. How moving, still, are the few monolithic pillars of the Temple of Hera which the Greeks, the least sentimental of peoples, piously left untouched in the very centre of Olympia where every generation did its best to outstrip its predecessors in the scale and sumptuousness of its rebuilding!

However, let us at once admit that such sentiments should be kept strictly within bounds, and never, never exploited for propaganda purposes. The classic and most terrifying example of what is likely to happen if such considerations are disregarded is provided by the present state of Rome. Here during the Fascist régime accumulations of the architectural relics of ten centuries—many of them incidentally evocative in the highest degree of true piety—were too often ruthlessly swept aside in order to expose some dreary symbol of a vulgar past in the vain hope of stimulating enthusiasm for an even more vulgar present. While we may be right in thinking that we are temperamentally inhibited from such ridiculous performances, we may yet fall into the same error from sentimentality or misplaced enthusiasm for the archaic.

Of all three of our grounds for defence that of scenic usefulness is the most difficult upon which to take a stand and by no means the least important. For the number of people who consciously realise the vital part played by one small unit in landscape or an architectural

◈◈◈◈◈◈◈◈◈◈◈◈◈◈◈◈◈◈◈◈◈◈◈◈◈◈◈◈◈◈◈

ensemble from which they consciously derive pleasure is always very small. Conscious awareness only comes, alas, when the effect has been ruined by the disappearance of the unit in question. It is, largely, a matter of scale and contrast and as such not amenable to generalisation, but nowhere can it be studied to better advantage than in New York. Owing to curtain-walling and other contemporary building methods, and the vastness of the scale, while a modern office block may well be an architectural masterpiece if viewed in isolation (which it most certainly never will be), when flanked and faced by other office blocks, conceived in the same idiom, it becomes an anonymous bore. But on the other hand even a comparatively undistinguished example alongside an old brownstone or a bit of General Grant Gothic, acquires a certain vitality and may well achieve a visual interest beyond that originally envisaged by the architect. While still dominated by the Tower of Grand Central the landscape of Park Avenue not only survived, but was enhanced by, the erection of the more recent skyscrapers; now, owing to the siting of the Pan-Am building, the period exuberance of the Tower itself has been rendered completely ineffective, the contrast shattered, and what was the best urban vista in New York has become as claustrophobic and as unexciting as the bottom of a lift-shaft.

That the building to be preserved for these reasons is not itself of any great merit is beside the point; its function in the scheme of things has become quite different from its original one and such considerations are, therefore, pointless.

Similarly there are certain, though rarer, cases where a misplaced enthusiasm for preservation at all costs can, by the elimination of the natural landscape background, rob a monument of most of its visual significance. It is this fact which renders the transportation and re-erection of historic buildings so chancy a procedure and will almost certainly nullify the current scheme for saving the temples at Abu Simbel. Considered in isolation these latter are almost wholly without aesthetic merit, the ham-fisted expression of a tedious megalomania; their only value is dependent on their relationship to the Nile and the surrounding hills, and once removed their aesthetic inadequacy will become glaringly apparent for the short period during which, given the prevailing wind, they are likely to survive on a new site.

Having thus briefly considered the only three arguments for preservation which seem to me justifiable, I should like to discuss one that I do not. No building lacking aesthetic merit, not evoking a genuine *piety*, and playing no part in the landscape should be allowed to occupy a site needed for something else solely on the grounds that it is unique. One of the few indisputable benefits which modern science has afforded us is that of making full

161

and accurate records. Therefore it is not sufficient to say that this stretch of wall must be preserved because it is the only existing example of such and such a form of bonding dating from the Roman occupation. So what? we can reply. Now that we know that the Romans did build in this particular way, measure it, photograph it, and pull it down. For in order to preserve what should be preserved we must, at all costs, be clearheaded about our motives. We must realise that we are deeply thankful that Westminster Hall escaped the bombing not because it is the largest fourteenth-century open timber roof in the world, but because it is a work of supreme architectural merit, deeply embedded at the very heart of English history, playing a vital role in the architectural ensemble of Parliament, St. Margaret's, and the Abbey.

Having thus inadequately defined the grounds on which we are entitled to preserve, it is necessary shortly to consider how preservation should be undertaken. This is the more difficult owing to the virtual impossibility of generalising; every old building presents peculiar problems and demands individual treatment. One can, therefore, only attempt to define the rough outline of the problem and confine oneself to the negative role of saying what on no account must be done.

Architecture, unlike painting and to a certain extent sculpture, does, save in the absolute sense, exist in time. It suffers the effect of wind and weather, and the additions and alterations of man. It may be frozen music, but it melts. And this process is by no means invariably a disadvantage, and its operation should always be foreseen by architects; for at a certain point in time even the greatest architecture ceases to be completely architecture and becomes partially landscape. Sometimes the wheel at last turns full circle; the pyramids are now wholly landscape, Stonehenge but faintly architecture. It follows logically, therefore, that any attempt to arrest this process is to go against the natural order, and that preservation should aim at doing no more than maintaining a building in a state in which it is still capable of being subject to this long transformation. One cannot, and should never attempt, to put the hands back or even to stop the clock by arbitrarily selecting one stage of this process and crying halt.

Most frequently such attempts are made on the specious plea of "restoring a building to its original state". Quite apart from the virtual impossibility of ever achieving this goal, in striving to do so we risk in almost all cases the total destruction of its existing contemporary value. For architecture is not in the same sense as painting and sculpture a pure art, and therefore alone of the visual arts cannot survive in a museum. Once it fulfils no function save the purely aesthetic, a virtue goes out of it and the sooner it becomes landscape, that is falls into ruin, the better. To illustrate what I mean I can do no better than to cite the case of one of the most celebrated of all the world's buildings. The Church of the Divine Wisdom at Constantinople remained a place of worship for orthodox Christians for over 700 years, and for 500 more as the Mosque of the Prophet fulfilled the same role for the Moslems. Now as Santa Sophia it is a national monument. To be unimpressed by this stupendous building would be impossible, the beauty of the end is so perfectly matched by the incredible boldness of the means; but one is nevertheless aware, not so much of a disappointment, as of a tiny lack, of which those who knew it in its days as a mosque were never conscious. Someone—in fact the late Ataturk—has cried "halt" and the natural cycle has been interrupted. For a building such as this can easily withstand a change of function within limits, but not a total suspension of function. One is aware of no such mixed feelings on entering the great Mosque at Famagusta, of infinitely less merit architecturally but still as fine an example of late thirteenth-century French Gothic as you will find outside the Ile-de-France, whose bare whitewashed interior is quite empty save for the *mihrab*, the *mimba*, and the prayer rugs beamed on Mecca, and from whose engargoyled towers the muezzin so surprisingly summons. For it is a far, far better thing for the House of God to fall into the hands of the infidel than to pass into the keeping of a Government Department.

Nor does one feel any sense of disappointment at the total absence of purpose displayed by the Parthenon, for the reward of all good architecture—and even of some bad—of becoming in part landscape has long ago been accorded it. But elsewhere on the Acropolis one does; from the little temple of Nike Apteros, so carefully, so conscientiously, put together by the archaeologist there does, for me at least, emerge just a faint discouraging whiff of the museum. Just how far one can go in this type of restoration—structurally necessary to some extent even to preserve ruins as landscape—is a very difficult question to answer. I never saw the Parthenon before the much criticised re-erection of the north colonnade, and I am bound to confess am conscious of experiencing no lack of intensity, no falling off, on seeing it in its present state. But it does create what I feel to be a dangerous precedent. Ridiculous as was that great architect Schinkel's ingenious and wildly theatrical scheme to absorb all the ruins on the Acropolis into a tasteful new palace for his patron, King Otho, elaborately published but never, mercifully, carried out, I am not wholly certain that it was not, in theory at any rate, preferable to the dehydrated archaeological approach. And I most certainly regret the disappearance of the Frankish tower which stood alongside the Propylaea well into the middle of the last century.

There is, however, one exception to this ban on total restoration, and it will, I trust, serve to prove the rule. One is only justified in attempting to re-create a building in its original state if these conditions are fulfilled: if one has a truly accurate idea of what its original state, in fact, was; if all continuity between that state and the present has been broken; and if it plays no part in the surrounding landscape. And it is very, very seldom that these three circumstances exist in combination. For example, in the case of the Temple of Nike, or better still the Treasury of the Athenians at Delphi, thanks to Greek methods of stonecutting during this period it has been possible to use most of the original stones in their original positions, so that our first condition, save in the matter of colour, is fully met. In addition, thanks to the fact that the very site of Delphi was lost for centuries beneath a mountain village, no sense of continuity is outraged. But, so far from helping the existing landscape, in this case the other ruins, it not only serves to mar it but is itself rendered slightly ridiculous by it. One needs to make not a smaller, but a greater effort of imagination to relate a building which at first sight in those surroundings looks like a tastefully designed custodian's lodge to one's idea of Delphi as a whole.

On the other hand, such sites as Carcassonne, Caernarvon, or Nuremberg fail for different reasons. The available knowledge of their original appearance did not amount to certainty and the imagination of the architect was called in. But not, alas, his creative imagination; only a fumbling, frightened groping for the past. And, moreover, continuity did exist and was disregarded, with the result, particularly at Nuremberg, that one never for a moment felt that the old town bore any relation to the rest of the city, but existed at its heart like the historical section of some international exhibition. How infinitely preferable was Wyatville's treatment of Windsor: its pretentions to genuineness  would hardly deceive a four-year-old, but how completely and how soon has it become a part of the landscape in its own right! And this is largely due to the fact that Wyatville has obeyed the instructions which in my youth I so constantly received from my old piano teacher: "If you can't be accurate, dear, at least you can strike the wrong note boldly." Would that all restorers would bear this in mind!

In the case of the Byzantine churches of Ravenna, however, which have recently been elaborately restored, I do feel that our three conditions are in fact fulfilled. Owing to the nature of mosaic, which is of all media the least subject to the ravages of time, and the most easy by modern methods accurately to replace, we are here in no doubt as to the rightness of our conception of the past. As the majority of them are hidden away by modern buildings and all save S. Apollinaire in Classe inconspicuous, the landscape, which anyhow in this part of the Adriatic seaboard changes quicker than the architecture, is not affected. But, most important—and in this Ravenna is unique among Italian cities—the continuity of life has been virtually broken. Elsewhere, as at Rome or Florence, most of our pleasure derives from the complete integration of past and present. The poster advertising the charms of Claudia Cardinale or Campari bitters flapping alongside the Renaissance doorway in the Romanesque façade does not distress us, and we accept the abominable Vespas skidding round the base of Michelangelo's David because both are equally manifestations of the Italian genius. But at Ravenna this continuity does not exist; between the city of Theodoric and the modern town there is no link. The monuments of the former are far further removed from present-day Ravenna than the streets of Pompei from the slums of

Naples. So infinitely remote is everything symbolised by the mosaics, so far away does Byzantium seem, that in San Vitale I even resent the presence of the trivial rococo ceiling painting, whereas elsewhere such traces of the intervening years, the presence of the baroque wall tablet above the tortoise stove between the fifteenth-century rood screen and the Victorian glass, are among the chief sources of my pleasure in old churches.

In England, however (and this is true to an even greater degree in America), there is not the superabundance of great large-scale masterpieces which exist in Italy or France, and one would like to think that those we have are safe. (Unfortunately what with the Senate's tinkering with the Capitol in Washington and the reckless treatment of the skyline round St. Paul's in London, such optimism may not, it seems, be wholly justified.) The major problem with which preservationists are faced, is,

GEO. REX FID. DEF. MDCCXX

ON THIS SITE WILL BE ERECTED THE MAGNIFICENT NEW PREMISES OF THE PROSCENE DEVELOPMENT CO

therefore, the saving of innumerable examples of first-rate but unspectacular buildings, architecturally of no less merit in their own degree than the great bravura set-pieces, but for which it is far more difficult to drum up sympathy or consideration.

In our present circumstances almost every county in England has five times as many fine eighteenth-century country houses alone as can possibly be supported in the conditions to which they are accustomed. And in America the same problem arises, if in a less acute form, in parts of New England, the Southern states and along the Hudson. Apart from the very, very tiny minority which, with or without the aid of the National Trust, can continue to fulfil their original function, how far can their value survive conversion into schools, lunatic asylums or government offices? Insofar as their interiors are concerned, hardly at all. Inclusion in a museum may be the kiss of death, but it is only a death of the spirit. Conversion into a reform school means physical annihilation as well. They must depend, therefore, for their survival upon the merits of their exteriors and their value in the landscape. So long as these can be preserved, do what you will with the interiors; if they cannot, remove the roof and let them fall into ruin.

In towns, on the other hand, in striving to save the whole we too often lose the chance of preserving the most valuable part, the façade. A chain store, let us say, buys a corner site in a market town occupied by a pleasant eighteenth-century brick or clapboarded building, not particularly distinctive in itself but playing a vital role in the general effect of the town centre. A few enthusiasts, knowing only too well the feast of chromium and black glass which is shortly to be theirs, start an agitation. If this is sufficiently powerful they may, in England, persuade the local authorities to schedule the building under the Town and Country Planning Act as being of architectural or historic interest, and to make an order for its preservation which will, while it is in force, effectively prevent demolition or alteration. Two years then pass during which the purchasers do nothing with their property, windows get broken, rain and decay set in. They then return to the charge pleading that the premises are now utterly incapable of any sort of conversion short of a total demolition, and this time, with the support of the local councillors who feel that the derelict at the heart of the town is bad for trade, win their case, and the order is revoked. Now, if at the beginning a preservation order had been issued for the façade alone, agreement could probably have been reached. In France, where this procedure is customary, the most striking monument to its effectiveness is perhaps the Ritz Hotel in Paris. Here the hotel company were allowed to do whatever interior remodelling they wished but were forbidden to alter so much as a single moulding on the façade. A compromise which has given complete satisfaction to all parties.

Finally a word to the unconverted; those who hold that the backward glance is not only unnecessary but positively dangerous. That a preoccupation with the past is a foolishness which less reactionary, more forward-looking peoples should eschew. Aligning themselves in fact with the late lamented Signor Marinetti, and repeating, albeit perhaps unconsciously, the sentiments so powerfully expressed in the Futurist Manifesto, they cry for a clean slate.

Let me remind them that, no matter how contemporary you strive to be, scratch as a starting point is forever unattainable. That whereas it remains questionable whether we do mount on our dead selves to higher things, it is certain that we can get nowhere if we reject the assistance afforded by the experience of our forebears. Without the continuous deposits of architectural humus no modern architecture can thrive, and if we scrape away the topsoil it will inevitably wither away. For no matter how clearly we envisage our objectives, no one can build the New Jerusalem in a cultural dustbowl.

The complete text for this section is provided by Osbert Lancaster's lecture on stage design, which I believe to be unpublished. It is illuminating because it is so much the work of a pragmatist, in a man without grandiose theories who was interested chiefly in finding the right solutions for the immediate problems in hand. The illustrations include set designs and costume studies for some of his best known productions. Unlike much modern work of this sort they are delightful simply as drawings, as well as providing an excellent guide to what was to be created on stage. Few better designers for opera and ballet have existed since the golden era of Diaghilev.

STAGE DESIGN

ON STAGE DESIGN

Lecture given at Rosehill Opera House, Whitehaven, Cumberland, 1964

IT IS the first duty of everyone connected with a theatrical production to induce in the audience a suspension of disbelief. For unless this is achieved and sustained they might just as well be at home with a good book. The customers, who are presumably of average intelligence, will be fully aware that when the overture starts they are more or less comfortably installed in the grand tier at Covent Garden, or wherever they happen to be sitting, and that outside lorries are unpacking vegetables, neon lights are flickering, and the twentieth century is displaying all its contemporary charms, but as soon as the curtain rises they must be transported to the bottom of the Rhine, or a wood near Athens, or the Tap Room of the Garter Inn. If the production is a really great one, and this, as we all know, does not happen every day, this suspension of disbelief will continue into the interval, and for a moment or two it will seem that it is not the battlements of Elsinore which are unreal, but the Foyer bar; and we sip our gin and tonics with certain apprehension, suspecting poison or love-filters.

To achieve such a result will have demanded a maximum degree of co-operation between producer, designer, and actors, and in the case of an opera—the conductor. But in so far as human beings tend to base their judgements first of all on what they see, and then on what they hear, the designer's role is, in this respect, if in no other, initially the most important. Occasionally in an opera the composer will have made his task easier by providing an overture; but when the curtain rises it is with the designer that the responsibility for the initial impact rests. As Stendhal said in his biography of Rossini:

> "Rien ne dispose mieux à être touché par la musique que ce leger frémissement de plaisir que l'on sent à la Scala au lever de la toile, à la première vue d'une décoration magnifique."

How then is the designer to set about this extremely difficult operation?

First of all, he must never forget that while it may well be, as many have claimed, the function of the stage to hold a mirror up to nature, it must be not only like Alice's Looking Glass, one through which one has the illusion that one can freely pass, but also equipped with a lens, magnifying and slightly over-emphasising everything which it reflects. Everything must be slightly larger, brighter, or more sombre than in life. A traditional proof of this necessity is embodied in the old theatrical superstition which deems it unlucky ever to have real flowers on the stage, an unconscious realisation of the fact that even the most magnificent hothouse blooms appear unconvincing and faintly sloppy when theatrically lit. Personally, I am of the opinion that this rule holds good even in plays which are avowedly naturalistic. Hedda Gabler's drawing-room must always be just that one degree stuffier and more oppressive in its decoration and furnishing than anything one could have found in real life, even in nineteenth-century Bergen.

In their non-acceptance of this truth, and in this only, I feel that Stanislavsky and the Moscow Art Theatre were at fault in their productions of Chekhov. While complete naturalism may well be unattainable if not wholly acceptable in interiors, Chekhov so frequently sets important scenes out of doors, in a lakeside garden, or a birch grove, and for me, watching the Moscow Art Theatre's production of *The Three Sisters* the moment

169

when the suspension of disbelief becomes no longer possible is in the last scene with those realistic birch trees waving unconvincingly over a stage littered with real autumn leaves.

If these considerations are valid on the theatrical stage, they apply even more forcibly in an opera or ballet. If *La Dame aux Camélias* must be thought to be coughing up one lung, *La Traviata* must convince us that she is coughing up two. If, in *The Merry Wives of Windsor*, Hearne's oak must be larger, older, and more sinister than any tree to be found in Windsor Forest, then in *Falstaff* it must be a veritable Yggdrasil. However, in deciding just how far he can go, and exactly what are the best methods of achieving his aims, the designer will not in most cases be forced to come to a decision unaided, as the producer is likely, quite rightly, to have ideas of his own. It is at this point, perhaps, that I should say a few words about the producer–designer relationship.

First, it must be assumed that the producer is already familiar with the designer's work, else he would not have chosen him, and that the designer has a respect and understanding for the producer's aims, else he would not have accepted. But this assumption is not always one hundred per cent safe, and some of the most disastrous productions of our time have been the outcome of either a designer being foisted on to a weak producer by the manager, or of a designer, eager for the job, agreeing to work with a producer whom he knows to be fundamentally unsympathetic.

However, assuming that the personal relationship is satisfactory, the most important thing, from the designer's point of view, is to understand exactly what the producer has in mind, and it is up to the producer to make perfectly clear the effects he wishes to achieve, the methods he intends to employ, and his personal conception of the work as a whole. One of the most difficult situations arises when the producer has not got any very clear idea of exactly what he wants, and expects the designer to make up his mind for him by producing various alternatives from which he can choose, or simply leaves the whole visual side entirely in the designer's hands. Almost as bad, and alas, more frequent, is the producer who has all too clear a picture of exactly what he wants, but is incapable of conveying his vision to the designer; in this case, the difficulty is heavily reinforced if the former has produced the work in hand somewhere else; for few things are more discouraging for a designer to hear than a muffled groan at the dress rehearsal, and to be told how staggering the effect of this particular scene was in the Turin production in 1935—a performance which the unfortunate designer never saw, despite its epoch-making success, but of which it is clear that his own efforts fall so lamentably short. Normally, these pitfalls can be avoided, providing the designer and producer get together early enough, and if the designer is prepared to do a sufficient number of preliminary sketches and models. Occasionally, however, difficulties may arise, particularly in the case of a busy and successful producer, from too long an interval having elapsed between preliminary consultations and the first rehearsals. For instance, I well remember one occasion when we had both gone into every possible detail of a particular scene and I had left the producer with a full set of roughs, sketches, photographs, and models, etc., and being greeted on stage at the first rehearsal by distraught screams, as the producer surveyed a painted staircase on the back-cloth. For although we had agreed a hundred times that this staircase must, for various technical reasons, be a painted one, in the period since our last meeting, it had taken on—in his imagination—a third dimension, and his whole conception of the scene now hinged upon everyone in the chorus marching up and down it. But the faults are by no means invariably all on one side, and few things can be more maddening for the producer than to discover at the first rehearsal that the open sward in the forest scene on which he had planned to have the whole Corps de Ballet disport themselves has been encumbered since he last saw the model with a small Greek temple or a Chinese folly, which the designer had subsequently felt would be an additional improvement, but had neglected to mention to the producer.

However, assuming that the producer and designer have established a united front, one of the first problems they will have to face, anyhow in opera, is that of period. You may well think that the solution is in most cases obvious and accepted, but I assure you that, for reasons I shall try to explain, it is far more complicated than that. In so far as opera is concerned, almost the only occasion on which the problem does not arise is in the case of contemporary operas on contemporary themes, works such as *The Consul* or *La Voix Humaine*—but such works, as you are doubtless aware, form but a tiny minority of the repertoire. Then come works which are now historical but were contemporary when they were written—*The Marriage of Figaro* and *La Traviata* are classic examples. For Mozart and Verdi, Count Almaviva and Violetta were contemporary figures involved in a purely contemporary situation, and to whom no period flavour attached. In such cases, I am convinced that the designer's job is, while keeping his characters in as accurate as possible reproduction of the period costume—for any attempt to play either piece in modern dress would be a tiresome piece of gimmickry—to eliminate any touch of fantasy or period whimsy. This is particularly so in the case of *Figaro* where, alas, the opposite is all too frequently tried on—for anything which softens the impact of what for Beaumarchais and Mozart was an essentially tough statement about the world in which they lived is to be deplored. *Figaro* is not, as so many productions imply, just a jolly romp to its delightful tunes, but a great deal more.

But the vast majority of operas, both ancient and modern, have historical settings, and it is here that the real difficulties arise. The problem is a double one: how far is the designer justified in adopting what I can only describe as a period-period type of approach? For he is forced to take into consideration not only the period in which the opera is actually set, but the idea of that period current at the time the opera was written.

Let me give you a familiar example. The action of Donizetti's *Lucia di Lammermoor* takes place in seventeenth-century Scotland as it was visualised by an Italian Romantic through the eyes of Sir Walter Scott, and to ignore this fact scenically would be to establish a most undesirable contradiction between sets and music. Personally, I thought that Signor Zeffirelli's recent production at Covent Garden was in this respect remarkably successful; without attempting to reproduce the mechanics or scenic effects of an Italian production of Donizetti's day, he contrived to re-create in theatrical terms the vision which had inspired so many romantic artists and illustrators. There are, however, dangers in this approach, which can all too easily be overdone. In the same producer's presentation of another Donizetti opera *Elisir d'Amore* at Glyndebourne, the period-period element was, to my mind, definitely overstressed; the first impact of the penny-plain, tuppence-coloured sets was delightful, but after a short while, their inadequacy became apparent. One scene would have made a delightful number in a Cochran revue, but the same treatment extended over three acts induced tedium. It is all very well, and in many cases essential, to put across period atmosphere, but dangerous to try to reproduce actual period mechanics.

Sketch for *Pineapple Poll*, Osbert Lancaster's first opera design, Sadler's Wells 1951.

Designs for *Falstaff*,
Glyndebourne, 1955

Cover design for the 1960 Glyndebourne programme

Costumes for *L'italiana in Algeri*,
Glyndebourne 1957

"La Pietra del Paragone" Glyndebourne 1964.   for George from Osbert 21

In no group of works is this problem of period so vexed as in those eighteenth-century operas dealing with classical themes—is the designer to clothe his Roman Emperors in the wreaths and togas which archaeological research tells us they actually wore; is he to put them in the full-bottomed wigs of the baroque tradition; or is he to try to evolve some contemporary fantasy on a classical basis? All three approaches have been tried with varying degrees of success. The first, though comparatively safe, is apt to be dull and has come to be regarded as old-fashioned. The second is occasionally justifiable but must be handled with care and considerable historical awareness. The most disastrous example of the second alternative that I have ever seen was the recent Balanchine production of Gluck's *Orpheo* at Hamburg. This was conceived on the most lavish possible scale. The whole action takes place in a vast half-circle of boxes inspired by the Court Theatre at Versailles, in which a chorus of courtiers in eighteenth-century classical fancy dress from time to time disported themselves; quite apart from the sheer ugliness of the set, the whole enterprise was doomed on two grounds. Firstly, the whole period had been pushed back nearly a century for no justifiable reason, for Gluck was a contemporary of Louis the Sixteenth, not the Fourteenth; and secondly, the composer has himself left on record that his whole object was to create a new art form and to rescue opera from the old tradition of the court masque, in which Balanchine was so anachronistically re-embalming it.

On the other hand, this approach has been tried out with considerable success in Handelian opera. The third alternative—that of making some contemporary comments on a classical theme—has on many occasions been brilliantly successful. One, many years ago, was the Cochran production of *La Belle Hélène* in which Mr. Oliver Messel enjoyed his first great success as a designer; a second, which ran in London and then new York—*A Funny Thing Happened on the Way to the Forum*—where Tony Walton's sets and costumes seemed to me to strike exactly the right note of fantasy without being facetious. It is, however, significant that both examples are comedies. It is doubtful whether this approach would succeed with *Julius Caesar*, and there were moments in the otherwise wonderful *Mr. Poppaea* when one or two of the costumes came near to crossing the borderline between fantasy and farce. When applied to works that are not just classical in inspiration but also in authorship, it is far more risky but can be amazingly effective. The Greek National Theatre's production of Aristophanes' *The Birds* struck me as being one of the most brilliantly successful examples of what the Germans call a *Gesamtkunstwerk* I have ever seen. The wonderfully imaginative and beautiful costumes, and economical but suggestive set by Tsaroukis, exactly matched the production, the extraordinarily inventive choreography, and the charming music based on modern Greek pop songs by the composer of *Never on Sunday*. If, as I believe likely, the Greek National Theatre returns to the Aldwych next year with this production, I beg you all to make every effort to see it.

Curiously enough, a quite different type of problem is presented by works which were once, even in our own lifetime, contemporary, but may by now have taken on a period flavour—*Madame Butterfly* for instance was, within living memory, the fearless operatic treatment of a contemporary theme, but neither Yokohama, nor the American Navy, are quite what they were in the days of Kokosan and Captain Pinkerton! And it would be manifestly impossible to bring that opera visually up to date. That this is always a dangerous proceeding is well demonstrated I think by the Sadler's Wells production of Kurt Weill's

Backcloth to *The Rising of the Moon*, Glyndebourne 1970.

Mahagonny, for although this was an outrageously avant-garde masterpiece, well within the memory of most of us here, it is today so essentially the product of a particular though short era, the last years of the Weimar Republic, that the blown-up photographs of Khrushchev and Kennedy, etc., and the Ban-the-Bomb placards, jarred as total irrelevances, reducing the whole production to the level of a contemporary Marxist tract.

Finally, there are certain works, and these perhaps produce the biggest headaches of all for the designer, of which the setting is not firmly anchored in time or space; the classic example is, of course, *The Magic Flute,* of which I have yet to see a wholly satisfactory production. Personally, I thought that Signor Enriques' treatment in last year's Glyndebourne production came nearest to success. At least by concentrating on the pantomime element and adopting a completely non-realistic, almost a child's picture-book technique for the scenery, he spared us the neo-classic boredom and masonic mummery which makes so many of the scenes in Sarastro's Agapemone, despite the wonder of the music, so inexpressibly tedious. Another and very different work which sets a somewhat similar problem is *Pelléas et Mélisande* but here the music comes to the designer's aid. Every bar calls to mind the mysterious greeny yellowy world of Burne-Jones, or rather perhaps that of the Nabis, that strange group of Parisian painters who were Debussy's contemporaries. This raises the question of the second great relationship in opera—that of the composer and designer. How much musical knowledge ought a designer working on an opera to possess? In the old days, the question hardly arose, for if he was engaged on an unfamiliar work unless—which was very unlikely—he could read a score, he would virtually know nothing of the music until rehearsals had started, when it would be far too late for him to gain any help from it, but with the coming of the gramophone, all that has changed, and I would always strongly advise any designer, even one whose musical education has been as sparse as mine, to play over a recording of the work as many times as possible. For there are some works where the composer has said so much about the setting in his score that the designer's task must be one of self-effacement. *Falstaff* is a good example; others where he has concentrated almost exclusively on the characters, or has contented himself with providing a string of rattling good tunes, and it is up to the designer to provide a visual equivalent of what, presumably, he had in mind.

So much for theory. However, there are one or two more practical relationships which an efficient designer must establish—first with the technicians—scene-painter, carpenter, and man on the lights. Which of these would be the most important will depend not only on the work in production, but also on the tradition in which the designer is working. By and large, there are three main schools of theatrical design; the oldest is that which relies principally upon painted canvas, a system which goes well back into the eighteenth century, when it was brought to a staggering degree of accomplishment by such artists as the Bibbiena family working in Bologna. It dominated stage design throughout most of the nineteenth century, becoming steadily more insipid, and was revived at the beginning of the present century by such designers as Bakst, and Benois, whose debt to the Bibbienas was open and avowed. After the First World War it was given an entirely new change of direction thanks to the genius of Diaghilev, who enrolled in the service of the theatre such leading contemporary painters as Picasso, Chirico, and Marie Laurencin.

Secondly, there is what might justifiably be described as the architectural school, which developed towards the end of the nineteenth century, and relied for its effects on solid three-dimensional sets. The most notable practitioner in this style between the wars was perhaps Professor Ernst Stern, who was responsible for innumerable productions at the Vienna Opera, and whose most notable work in this country was done for Noël Coward's *Bitter Sweet*; today, this tradition is stoutly maintained by Monsieur Mahkevitch.

Lastly, there is the tradition which may be said to have originated with Gordon Craig, which relies enormously on lighting for its effects, but which has always been more popular in Germany and central Europe than here, and which tends to avoid realism in favour of atmospheric suggestion. Which method or combination of methods the designer chooses will be governed not only by his own preferences, but also by the equipment of the theatre in which he is working. On the whole, British theatres are, by continental standards, old-fashioned in design and inadequate in equipment. In London, there is only one theatre where the grid is sufficiently high to render the use of sky-boarders unnecessary, and that one—needless to say—has been changed into a cinema. On the Continent, sky-boarders are practically unknown; similarly, there are, I believe, only two theatres in London equipped with a revolve, and as this means that all the scenery has to be manhandled on and off the stage during the performance, the amount of heavy built pieces will be strictly limited by the storage space available in the wings. Similarly, in the absence of a cyclorama—which in the English theatre are few and far between—the designer would be ill-advised to rely too heavily on ambitious lighting effects. In this connection a further difficulty arises, although more frequently in the commercial theatre than in opera, owing to the custom of touring a new production in the provinces before opening in London. The unfortunate designer who has been told that the curtain will rise at some London theatre of moderate size—the Adelphi, or the Strand—and has worked out all his designs on that groundplan, will suddenly be told at the last moment that before going to London the production will open, say, at the King's Theatre in Edinburgh—a very small stage with a steep rake—and will then play for a week at Oxford where the proscenium opening is the widest in England, and that somehow all his sets will have to be adjusted to suit the local conditions. However, these comparative difficulties under which the English designer works are not wholly disadvantageous because a great deal of elaborate equipment has its dangers. In Vienna, for instance, it is on such a scale and so complicated that most producers are too scared to use it at all; elsewhere the designer is encouraged to modify his designs to show off the various technical tricks made possible by the stage machinery.

Finally, there is the designer's relationship with the cast. This naturally is principally governed by questions of costume and make-up, and will call for a high degree of tact and persuasiveness to maintain on an even keel. Most singers are intensely conservative and will always wish to wear what they have worn before, or something like it. It is no unusual thing for a foreign prima donna to arrive with a full set of costumes which she wore when she last sang the role in Berlin or Milan, and to be exceedingly affronted on being told that they cannot easily be accommodated in the current production. But it is not only sopranos who make these little difficulties. I once worked with a Spanish tenor, in all respects one of the most charming and co-operative of singers, who insisted, on superstitious grounds, that the little Peter Pan collar in *point de Venise* lace which he had worn when he enjoyed his first great success in the role of Edgardo in *Lucia* must be worked into whatever costume he happened to be singing in. While an ingenious and accommodating designer might be able to oblige in such roles as Fenton in *Falstaff*, as Captain Pinkerton the difficulties, one imagines, would have proved insuperable. There are of course certain operatic traditions which have now become so well established as to be acceptable.

182

It would, for instance, be a rash designer who attempted to alter Don Basilio's shovel hat. Others seem less justified, and I can well remember a ding-dong struggle I once had with an Italian soprano who maintained that to play Nanetta without long blonde plaits, for which her face, one could see at a glance, had not been designed by nature, was unthinkable. Usually, however, singers are more amenable to persuasion than might be imagined. Although if they have sung at the Met, they are always noticeably difficult to deal with and, in addition, there are always one or two members of the chorus who will declare that the lightest possible headdress or wig, if it comes within six inches of their ears, renders it quite impossible for them to hear the orchestra.

So much for costume; there remains the question of make-up. In England this is an art which has been grossly neglected. Every continental opera house and most theatres have a resident expert with staff who carry out the whole operation in accordance with the designer's request. In England, where in theory all actors and actresses have been trained to do it for themselves, the results are seldom encouraging; and, furthermore, when foreign singers come over, they sit hopefully waiting for the expert to appear, who usually turns out to be the wretched designer himself, faced with a long row of eyebrow pencils and greasepaint, which he has not the vaguest idea how to employ. Further difficulties are likely to arise from the burning resentment which so many members of the chorus feel at having to put on make-up at all, let alone to change it between roles, and their firm determination never to use body make-up at all. This of course makes things very difficult in those operas which call for bare torsos and gleaming thighs, when the wretched designer is forced to make do with thick woollen leotards covering body and limbs, and seldom—if ever—matching the greasepaint on the face. In this connection, I shall never forget a performance of *Aida* I once saw at the Paris Opera where all the chorus were dusky brown from neck to navel and wrist to shoulder, but with pale white faces and hands, and where one of the other ranks in the Egyptian Army had even neglected to remove his pince-nez.

In conclusion, there is just one other relationship of which I realise I have neglected to speak: it is that of the designer and the management—and in most cases is best conducted through a really good agent!

OSBERT LANCASTER 1908–1986

Lancaster, Sir Osbert, Kt 1975; RDI 1979; Hon. FRIBA; b. 4 August 1908; eldest son of Robert Lancaster and Clare Bracebridge Manger; m. 1933, Karen (d. 1964), d. of Sir Austin Harris, KBE; one s. one d.; m. 1967 Anne Scott-James; d. 27 June 1986.

Educ. Charterhouse and Lincoln College, Oxford (Hon. Fellow 1979); Slade School. Cartoonist *Daily Express* from 1939; Foreign Office (News Dept) 1940; attached to HM Embassy, Athens, 1944–6; Sydney Jones Lecturer in Art, Liverpool University, 1947. Adviser to GLC Historic Buildings Board, 1969–. Governor King Edward VII School, King's Lynn. Hon. D. Litt., Birmingham, 1964; Newcastle-upon-Tyne, 1970; St. Andrews, 1974; Oxford, 1975. Fellow University College London, 1967.

STAGE DESIGNS

Pineapple Poll, Sadler's Wells, 1951; *Bonne bouche*, Covent Garden, 1952; *Love in a Village*, English Opera Group, 1952; *High Spirits*, Hippodrome, 1953; *Rake's Progress*, Edinburgh (for Glyndebourne), 1953; *All's Well That Ends Well*, Old Vic, 1953; *Don Pasquale*, Sadler's Wells, 1954; *Coppelia*, Covent Garden, 1954; *Napoli*, Festival Ballet, 1954; *Falstaff*, Edinburgh (for Glyndebourne), 1955; *Hotel Paradiso*, Winter Garden, 1956; *Zuleika*, Saville, 1957; *L'italiana in Algeri*, Glyndebourne, 1957; *Tiresias*, English Opera Group, 1958; *Candide*, Saville, 1959; *La Fille mal gardée*, Covent Garden, 1960; *She Stoops to Conquer*, Old Vic, 1960; *La pietra del paragone*, Glyndebourne, 1964; *Peter Grimes*, Bulgarian National Opera, Sofia, 1964; *L'Heure espagnole*, Glyndebourne, 1966; *The Rising of the Moon*, Glyndebourne, 1970; *The Sorcerer*, D'Oyly-Carte, 1971.

PUBLICATIONS

Progress at Pelvis Bay (1936), *Our Sovereigns* (1936), *Pillar to Post* (1938), *Homes Sweet Homes* (1939), *Pocket Cartoons* (1940–3), *Assorted Sizes* (1944), *Classical Landscape with Figures* (1947), *The Saracen's Head* (1948), *Drayneflete Revealed* (1949), *Façades and Faces* (1950), *Lady Littlehampton and Friends* (1952), *All Done from Memory* (1953), *Studies from the Life* (1954), *Tableaux Vivants* (1955), *Private Views* (1956), *The Year of the Comet* (1957), *Etudes* (1958), *Here of All Places* (1958), *Signs of the Times* (1961), *Mixed Notices* (1963), *Graffiti* (1964), *A Few Quick Tricks* (1965), *Fasten Your Safety Belts* (1966), *With an Eye to the Future* (1967), *Temporary Diversions* (1968), *Sailing to Byzantium* (1969), *Recorded Live* (1970), *Meaningful Confrontations* (1971), *Theatre in the Flat* (1972), *The Littlehampton Bequest* (1973), *Liquid Assets* (1975), *A Cartoon History of Architecture* (1975), *The Social Contact* (1977), *The Pleasure Garden* (with Anne Scott-James) (1977), *Scene Changes* (1978), *Ominous Cracks* (1979), *The Life and Times of Maudie Littlehampton* (1982), *Night and Day* (with others) (1985).

ILLUSTRATIONS
AND ACKNOWLEDGEMENTS

Prelims: Coll. Lady Lancaster

2: Osbert Lancaster at home (Coll. Lady Lancaster)

4: The Tenor, *Friends of Covent Garden Magazine* (Coll. Lady Lancaster); **insert:** costume design for the chorus of *La pietra del paragone* (Christie's)

5–6: *Façades and Faces*

7: **Top:** Stage design for *La Fille mal gardée* (Coll. Lord Snowdon); **bottom left:** Village on the Nile (Coll. Michael Ginesi); **bottom right:** Egyptian Landscape (Coll. Lady Lancaster)

8: **Main picture:** costume design for chorus of *Falstaff* (Christie's); **top:** London Underground poster (London Transport Museum); **bottom:** costume designs for the chorus of *La pietra del paragone* (Christie's)

9: Cover for *The Ambassador* magazine (Coll. Lady Lancaster)

10: **Top left:** book jacket (Coll. Lady Lancaster); **top right:** book jacket (Coll. Michael Ginesi); **bottom:** book jacket (Coll. Lady Lancaster)

11: Book jacket (Coll. Lady Lancaster)

17: Illustrations from *All Done from Memory* and *With an Eye to the Future*

18: **Top:** Knighthood card (Coll. Lady Lancaster); **bottom:** Osbert Lancaster (Coll. Lady Lancaster)

20–33: *All Done from Memory*

36: *Classical Landscape with Figures*

39–42: *All Done from Memory*

43–4: *The Saracen's Head*

46: *All Done from Memory*

47: Page from an Egyptian Sketchbook (Coll. Lady Lancaster); **left:** cartoon from *Night and Day*; **centre:** illustration for book jacket, *4th Leaders from The Times* (Coll. Lady Lancaster)

49–50: *Façades and Faces*

51: *From an Italian Sketchbook*

52: *From an Italian Sketchbook*

53: Italian Scene (Coll. Lady Lancaster)

54: Italian Scene (Coll. Lady Lancaster)

55–6: *Façades and Faces*

57–8: The market place, Richelieu, from a French sketchbook (Coll. Lady Lancaster)

59: French sketchbooks (Coll. Lady Lancaster)

61–2: Greek Scene (Coll. Lady Lancaster)

63: **Top:** The Little Metropolis, Athens (Coll. Lady Lancaster); **bottom:** Vatopedi, Athos (Coll. Lady Lancaster)

64: **Top:** *Classical Landscape with Figures*; **bottom:** page from a Greek sketchbook (Coll. Lady Lancaster)

65–6: *Façades and Faces*

70–2: *Classical Landscape with Figures*

73: Great Lavra, Athos, from *Sailing to Byzantium*

75–6: Spetsai (Coll. Lady Lancaster); High Wind on Tenos (Coll. Lady Lancaster)

77: The Hen-House, Plataneia, from a Greek sketchbook (Coll. Lady Lancaster)

78: The White Mountains, from Ano Plataneia (Coll. Lady Lancaster)

79: Great Lavra, Athos, from *Sailing to Byzantium*

81: Illustration from a Greek sketchbook (Coll. Lady Lancaster)

83: Vatopedi, Athos, from *Sailing to Byzantium*

85: Aphendiko, Mistra, from *Sailing to Byzantium*

88: Coll. Lady Lancaster

89–90: Illustrations from an Egyptian sketchbook (Coll. Lady Lancaster)

91–2: *Façades and Faces*

93: **Top left:** illustration from *The Unbearable Bassington*; **top right:** illustration from *Drayneflete Revealed*; **bottom:** illustration for book jacket, *Oxford Now and Then*

94: **Top:** *Progress at Pelvis Bay*; **bottom:** *With an Eye to the Future*

95: *Keys to Understanding the English*

96–103: Sequence from *The Ambassador* magazine, 1953

104–6: Illustrations from *Keys to Understanding the English*

107–8: *Façades and Faces*

109–10: *The Pleasure Garden*

111–13: *Yoicks! or, The Fox Outfoxed*

115–18: *Daily Express* cartoons (courtesy John Murray Ltd)

119: **Top:** cartoon from *Cornhill Magazine*, 1947; **bottom:** After Breakfast at Kelmscott (Coll. Lady Lancaster)

120: The Whitbread Calendar, 1970 (Whitbread Brewery)

The publishers would like to thank the following people for their kind help in the compilation of this book: Mr John G. Murray, Mr Michael Ginesi, Sir Geraint Evans, Mr Septimus Waugh, Lord Snowdon, Mr George Malcolm Thompson and, above all, Lady Lancaster.